SHADOWS OF MEN

MW00655095

Kevin Grauke

SHADOWS OF MEN

Queen's Ferry Press

Queen's Ferry Press
8240 Preston Road
Suite 125-151
Plano, TX 75024
www.queensferrypress.com

The characters and events in this book are fictitious. Any similarity to real persons, living or dead, is entirely coincidental and not intended by the author.

Copyright © 2012 by Kevin Grauke

All rights reserved, except for brief quotations in critical articles or reviews. No part of this book may be reproduced in any manner without prior permission from the publisher: Queen's Ferry Press – 8240 Preston Road, Suite 125-151, Plano, TX 75024

Published 2012 by Queen's Ferry Press

Cover photo, "Staples and Nails," by Alan Whiteside

First edition December 2012

ISBN 978-1-938466-03-8

Printed in the United States of America

Praise for SHADOWS OF MEN:

"Kevin Grauke's elegant portrayals of introspective and fragile men recall John Updike's best work. This insightful and empathetic collection animates its characters' hearts so completely that they seem to beat within us. Taken as a whole these stories constitute a finely chiseled work of art."

—Tom Grimes, author of *Mentor: A Memoir*

"Kevin Grauke's *Shadows of Men* is a note-perfect, resonant new work. These stories have their fingers on strands of works by masters of the short story like Cheever, Dubus, and Ford, but consistently strike surprising and satisfying chords all their own. At turns hilarious and painful, dark and uplifting, these works speak genuinely to what it means to be a man in the world. It is the kind of work one delights in pushing onto friends to read and to read immediately."

—Darren DeFrain, author of *The Salt Palace* and *Inside & Out*

"Kevin Grauke is our post-Hemingway. *Shadows of Men* is *In Our Time* after the swamp has become a subdivision. Grauke writes from deep inside his fraught, clear-eyed protagonists, sons, fathers, and husbands who note that the women they love are more sure-footed in this hyper-domesticated landscape than they are. These men try to ignore the urge to fight, to secure, to pillage, to avenge, an urge made ridiculous, even pathological, by contemporary solutions to crisis. I read, holding my breath, hoping to see these men give in to pure instinct, meanwhile knowing that if they do they end up ruined. This funny, sad, and brave book refuses to simplify its exploration of heroism and its evil twin, savagery."

—Debra Monroe, author of *On the Outskirts of Normal*, *The Source of Trouble*, and *A Wild, Cold State*

"Kevin Grauke's *Shadows of Men* is a stunning debut story collection about our need to cling to and escape from the stories told about us. Grauke challenges us in each carefully etched line to question our assumptions about the nature of childhood, maleness, marriage, and fatherhood. Like William Trevor's or Richard Yates' wonderfully conflicted characters, Grauke's people are often caught wondering if they've settled into the skins they were meant for. *Shadows of Men*, like the best short story collections, reveals us to ourselves, surprising us again and again with its characters' half-forgotten urges, unspoken lines, and untended gardens, which are our own. A terrific, fearless piece of work."

—Scott Blackwood, author of *In the Shadow of Our House* and *We Agreed to Meet Just Here*

"Whether they find themselves hacking rattles from the tails of snakes or nesting rattles in the hands of their babies, the men Kevin Grauke has dreamed into life drift in the dim undercurrents of their own unrealized expectations. Page by page, *Shadows of Men* plumbs in equal measure the cold fathoms of masculine disappointment and the warm eddies of hope. To read these stories each by each is to hear the bruised, beating hearts thumping beneath the hard enamels of machismo. To read them all together is to be reminded that, while darkness lies in the absence of light, shadows are the muted proof that light exists, that the darkness may yet be dispelled."

—Bruce Machart, author of *The Wake of Forgiveness* and *Men in the Making*

For Catherine

It so happens that I am sick of my feet and my nails
and my hair and my shadow.
It so happens I am sick of being a man.

Still it would be marvelous
to terrify a law clerk with a cut lily,
or kill a nun with a blow on the ear.
It would be great
to go through the streets with a green knife
letting out yells until I died of the cold.

—From "Walking Around," by Pablo Neruda
(Translated by Robert Bly)

Table of Contents

The Limits of Adequacy	15
The Leaves, They Pirouette	41
Sub Rosa	46
Horsehead Crossing	68
The New Father	71
The Woods of Tawakoni	90
Congee	101
With the Snow	118
A Good Son	126
Out Here in the Fields (Again)	146
The Fading of Whittier	158
Welcome	173
Phenotypic	193

The Limits of Adequacy

I peer over my magazine at the other two men in the waiting room of the Gladstone Clinic, wondering if, like me, they've come to see how well their "boys can swim." That's how Dr. Victorino put it, in an unsuccessful attempt at lightening the mood. Neither appears to be even half as tense as me, though neither seems particularly interested in making eye contact, either. The guy reading *Sports Illustrated* has an expression on his face that reminds me of the happily lost look Julie gets whenever she's in the middle of rereading one of her Jane Austen novels from college. The guy in the ostrich cowboy boots, on the other hand, looks sleepy, as if he might doze off if his name doesn't get called soon.

The door next to the receptionist's frosted window opens, and a nurse with a tattoo on her forearm of something I can't make out—an alligator? a shark?—steps into view. Behind her, I can't see anything of the office's interior except a vivid cross section of a penis and scrotum framed in silver and hanging on the far wall.

"Mr. Fairweather?"

The guy reading *Sports Illustrated* doesn't look up as I walk past him. The cowboy's eyes droop shut.

Since Julie and I were both relatively young—thirty-two and thirty-three, respectively—and healthy when we started this, we assumed it wouldn't take us too long to get pregnant once she stopped taking the pill. Beyond agreeing that, yes, we were ready, we did nothing special. We'd accomplished nearly everything that we'd wanted to accomplish before moving on to this stage of our lives.

House? A nondescript but perfectly fine ranch home not too far from the freeway that Julie and everyone else living in Ivy hops on to get to work in downtown Dallas. Money in savings? More would have been nice, sure, but what we had was pretty good.

"Say goodbye to staying out until two on the weekends," Julie said as she ceremoniously threw her remaining birth control pills into the trash.

"Goodbye," I said, refusing to confess that I had grown tired of staying out until two on the weekends long ago.

Truth be told, I rarely notice children except when they call negative attention to themselves—throwing food in restaurants, running roughshod down the aisles of grocery stores. In these instances, I find myself mentally criticizing their parents for not being able to control them. Nevertheless, I'm confident that once I have my own it'll be a completely different story. As soon as my own child, still slick from the birthing, is placed in my arms there in the delivery room, I'll transform. The moment I look upon my child's face for the first time and see how its features have been cast from Julie's and mine, I'll become a different man. And it'll feel totally natural, rocking my child ever so gently back and forth, even though, at least as far as I can remember, I've never held an infant before. Over the years, whenever our friends have become new parents and asked if I'd like to hold Chase or Henry or Maya, I've always declined as they've pressed their progeny aggressively onto me, claiming to feel the flu coming on.

"I'd be afraid I might pass on whatever I've got," I say, when really what I'm afraid of is seeing the terror in their eyes as they watch me mishandle their swaddled bundle, sending it tumbling to the floor.

Not really knowing a better way to respond, each time that Julie told me she'd started her period, I said something along the lines of, *Oh, well, next month will be the month*. I was disappointed each time, sure, but not horribly, no. After all, what was a month? Just thirty days. Four weeks and change.

The sixth time she got her period, she said, "Well, it's been half a year now."

We were both in the kitchen when she said this, apropos of nothing. I was loading the dishwasher after dinner, thinking about whether to ask her if she wanted to take a walk around the block before it got too dark. She was sitting on a stool at the counter, flipping through a magazine.

"Since what?" I asked, though I knew.

"Since we started trying."

I couldn't tell whether she was just noting this fact or if she was concerned but trying to sound nonchalant, as if she'd only just suddenly realized this. "Already?"

"Tell me about it. But they don't even want to see me until we've been trying for a year, so I'm sure it's fairly normal . . . but still. Six months is six months, you know?"

I wondered who *they* were and how she happened to know this if she hadn't worriedly sought it out. Dropping a handful of forks and knives into the dishwasher's utensil basket, I thought about asking her if, in fact, she *was* worried, but already several seconds of silence had passed; to ask now I knew might cause her to think that my delay was rooted in an anxiety of my own regarding our inability to conceive, so I let it go.

Soon after this discussion, however, Julie became more aggressive. I didn't know why she chose the odd moments that she did to initiate sex, but I assumed it had something to do with the vagaries of her menstrual cycle. I enjoyed how she teasingly called from down the hall for her stud to come service her, though such explicit talk did embarrass me a bit, especially while sunlight was still pouring through the open windows. Playing along, I'd knock on the bedroom door and, in my best attempt at a suave voice, say, "Did someone here request a gigolo?"

Five more identical months passed. Julie didn't say anything more than to note the timely arrival of her period every fourth week or so, but I sensed the heightened anxiety underlying each successive announcement.

After the twelfth unsuccessful month, she said, "I'm going to get checked out next week."

Even though this comment broke ten minutes of silence between us one night as we sat together watching the news and eating a late snack of tortilla chips and guacamole, I didn't need to ask what she was talking about.

"Do you want some company?"

She shook her head, her mouth full. "It's only with Dr. Hammond-Greene. She said she's just going to be a little more thorough than when she gave me the okay to start trying in the first place. Then we'll go from there."

I didn't say anything as I removed a dot of guacamole from her chin with my finger. I wondered if we were on the verge of one of those moments that, once whatever it was that was going to happen had happened, we would look back upon and think, *Remember when we thought . . . ? Remember when we had no idea that . . . ?*

After her appointment the following Wednesday, she sat on the couch next to me with a shrug. "I'm fit as a fiddle. Her words, not mine. At least from what she can tell."

All this time I had just assumed that if a problem existed it would be with her, not me. After all, a woman's body—what with all its tubes and folds and cavities, its whirling hormones—had to be more prone to malfunction, didn't it? Now I felt stupid, like the last one in the office to get the joke. *Of course* it could be me to blame just as easily! "So now it's my turn, I guess, right?"

"She said we should've started with you, anyway. Men are simpler." She smiled. "Her words again, not mine."

I wonder if the tattooed nurse, who smells of disinfectant laced with flowery perfume, is snickering to herself at the thought of what I'm about to do. Or is escorting men to the collection room just another dull part of her humdrum routine?

She stops at a door marked *Private.* "Have you abstained for the last seventy-two hours, as directed?"

Unnerved by her direct gaze, I nod, afraid that my voice might come out sounding nervous.

She hands me a lidded cup sealed in loose plastic. "Magazines are available inside if you need them," she says in a voice that now sounds like the rehearsed singsong of a tour guide's. "Lubricant is intentionally not made available because it might contaminate the sample. When you've finished, take your sealed cup to the lab technician's window at the end of the hall." She pauses a beat. "And don't forget to turn the lock."

I wait until she disappears into a nearby room before opening the door. I don't know what I expected to find (a waterbed? soft music?), but it certainly isn't just an ordinary bathroom—and an uncomfortably chilly one, to boot—that the staff probably uses whenever patients aren't busy masturbating in it. After undoing my pants and pushing down my boxers (which I've recently switched to after Julie noted that my "tighty whities might be keeping things too warm down there"), I waddle over to the magazine stand next to the sink.

Despite the legitimately medical nature of the circumstances, a slight feeling of shame comes over me as I pull a *Playboy* from the rack and thumb through the slick pages of taut, glowing skin. Beachcombing blondes kicking through ocean foam. A squad of cheerleaders exercising beneath a goalpost in a variety of incomplete uniforms, pompons in hand. And then the centerfold: a blue-eyed brunette luxuriating on a hay bale, wearing only a red bandanna tied around her neck. A chaff of wheat dangles precariously from her moist lips. From her navel, a diamond piercing winks at me. Choosing her, I get started.

Sitting in my office at work, I'm supposed to be writing a report for my boss, but I haven't even turned on my computer yet. Instead I'm staring blankly at a crack in the wall next to the thermostat. When had it widened so much? In the morning, my results from the Gladstone Clinic will be in. It's just like being back in school, watching the teacher as she makes her leisurely way down the aisles of desks, dropping tests from her fingers: would I pass or fail? Have I been shooting blanks, as the stupid saying goes, all this time?

I look through my open door into the conference room across the hall where a birthday party is well underway. A group of my salesmen are standing around with plates of cake and laughing at Randall, the youngest of the lot, who's hurling his fists dramatically at an invisible foe while regaling the others with what is, undoubtedly, an account of yet another one of his drunken weekend escapades. Have any of them—fathers all, by my vague recollection, except for Randall—had any difficulty getting *their* wives pregnant? None, most likely, which doesn't seem right. Don't I have more to offer as a father than any of them? At least I don't think that getting into a fight in the stands at a Cowboys game is a badge of honor.

Having seen me watching him, Randall's arms freeze in mid-swing. "Come get some cake, man. Quit being so goddamned industrious."

I sit forward and pick up a pencil, my head still cloudy. For a moment I relish my authority, knowing that I could call Randall into my office and chew him out—even fire him—over anything I want, even something imagined, and Randall would have to take it without complaint, but all I say is, "Maybe later."

When Randall returns to his story, punching the air all the while, I call Julie to make sure she'll be able to come with me to get my results. I need her there to help me make sense of things.

The results—

Vol.: 1.4
Liq.: NL
Count: 21
Morph.: 55%
pH: NL
WBC: None
Fruc.: NL

After briefly looking over the printout with Julie, I return it to Dr. Victorino. Hoping to sound nonchalant, I ask, "So, what's the verdict?"

"Well," Dr. Victorino says, drawing the word out unhurriedly, "strictly speaking, everything falls within, or only just below, what's typically considered the limits of adequacy, as we in the profession say. Which is good, but several of these figures are definitely pushing the low end of normal. And a couple have pushed on through, if you know what I mean. By themselves, none of these numbers beg for radical concern, I don't think, but all together? I'm not sure. Maybe."

I look over at Julie, who raises her eyebrows and shrugs, as if to say, "Okay, so . . . ?"

Dr. Victorino unwraps a piece of gum and folds it into his mouth. "Ideally, what we'd like to see is at least three times the volume and at least five times the count, with a higher percentage of well-structured, forward-moving specimens. A good portion of your sperm, however, are either misshapen—two-headed, tiny-headed, two-tailed, short-tailed—or simply bad swimmers."

As I struggle to think of an appropriate question to ask, a vision of cartoon sperm—little tadpole creatures with stern eyes and determined mouths—comes to me. At first they are a steady armada cruising industriously along, but abruptly they start thrashing about, gasping for air and drowning, their deformed heads weighing them down.

This isn't even slightly fair. Isn't it cruel enough that I recently verified with a paint-stained ruler from the kitchen junk drawer that my penis, which I've always assumed to be on the small side, is officially an inch shorter than the reported world average? Isn't it cruel enough that something like three billion men around the globe, most of them probably wandering around hungry in third-world countries, are better equipped? Isn't it cruel enough to know that Julie, every time I reach my shallow depth, must bemoan her own cruel fate, as well? Now I have to add *this* to my shortcomings?

"Regardless," Dr. Victorino continues, stepping around his desk toward us, "it's time to make an appointment with an RE, certainly. I'd be happy to suggest one, of course."

"An RE?" I ask, only half-listening.

"A reproductive endocrinologist," Julie says, a syllable ahead of Dr. Victorino.

"Oh, okay. Sure."

Despite Julie's hand in mine as we leave Dr. Victorino's office, I feel as if I'm alone, as if I accidentally stepped into a closet instead of into the cheerful hallway that leads us back to the waiting area.

After poring over our records for several silent minutes, Dr. Przybylinski, the unsmiling RE recommended by Dr. Victorino, finally looks up and says, "The first thing we need to do is get *you*"—he stabs his pen in my direction while his face remains disconcertingly blank—"tested again, Mr. Fairweather. Then, depending on the results—I am not expecting significant differentiation, mind you, but single samples do not always provide us with an accurate picture—we will proceed cautiously. No reason to do anything drastic, not immediately. I am confident that I will have you expecting soon enough."

So I return to the Gladstone Clinic. The tattooed nurse repeats the same speech from my first visit after escorting me to the same bathroom, her eyes giving no indication that she remembers me. I also return to the brunette still reclining on the hay bale. Her name is Holly, I read in her profile, and she's from rural Georgia. She wants to go to law school. And have a big family. And just as I did the first time, with my eyes locked on her sun-warmed breasts so unabashedly bared beside what might be her very own father's tractor, I labor and strain. After several fruitless minutes, I begin to worry, and sweat. I pause, allowing my aching arm to relax for a moment. What if I can't do it? Will the nurses in the hall start making quizzical faces at each other, wordlessly asking, *What the hell's going on in there?* I flex my fingers and then start up again, trying to imagine Holly calling for me to come service her.

Just as I'm about to either cramp up or faint from exhaustion, it finally happens. After the spasms subside, I shakily screw on the lid, wash my hands, and belt up my pants. Relieved, I step out into the hall, aware of nothing but my semen pooled at the bottom of the clear cup, visible to anyone who cares to look as they pass by.

"The numbers are consistent," says Dr. Przybylinski over the phone a few days later. "Plenty of men with worse numbers get their wives pregnant, but that does not mean that your sperm is not the primary problem here. With no reproductive assistance, you might very well get your wife pregnant, but it also might take years. It also might *never* happen."

My hope that my first sample was merely an unfortunate fluke dies.

"Think of your sperm as students doing poorly in school," Dr. Przybylinski goes on to say. "Some are simply not cut out for it. Others are doing poorly because they are underachievers. They need a little extra assistance. A little tutoring, so to speak."

I can tell that he's proud of this analogy, but I don't especially like having my sperm called stupid and lazy, even if I know it's silly to take offense. After all, it isn't as if he's calling *me* stupid and lazy. But still. I hang up and call Julie at work. While I wait for her to pick up, I kick my office door shut just as I catch sight of Randall strutting down the hall with his tie slung over his shoulder.

"I almost wish the news were worse," Julie says. "At least then we'd know a little more about what we're dealing with."

"I know," I say, though I don't agree, taking at least some consolation from the fact that I might still be able to get my wife pregnant without Dr. Przybylinski there to handle it for me.

Dr. Przybylinski starts our treatment by putting Julie on Clomid, a mild fertility drug, which requires her to test her basal temperature and LH levels regularly in order to pinpoint her time of ovulation. All I know is this: except for the three days of the month that we screw like rabbits, as Julie likes to say while grabbing me by the belt and pulling me down on top of her (with two pillows under her butt to optimize the possibility of fertilization), the rest of our time together seems to consist primarily of Julie squinting at a thermometer, Julie peeing on OvuQuick sticks (with me waiting on the other side of the bathroom door), Julie scribbling inscrutable notations in a variety of colored inks on a calendar magneted to the refrigerator, or Julie telling me the most recent awful thing she's read that could happen once she finally does get pregnant, things with names that sound like wizard spells—*hyperemesis gravidarum*, *preeclampsia*, *hydramnios*. To top it off, the Clomid makes her grouchy, but since she doesn't seem to notice the change, I don't mention it because it would only make her grouchier.

"No problem," Dr. Przybylinski says after the fourth unproductive month. "Clomid is not a cure-all, not by itself. Frankly, I would have been surprised if we met with success so quickly, but stranger things have happened." He clears his throat. "May I make a suggestion?"

I feel Julie's fingernails dig into my palm; I sense that the aggressive optimism she's maintained since our first appointment with Dr. Przybylinski is fading quickly.

"Maybe you would benefit from an infertility support group as we move forward," Dr. Przybylinski says, his mouth barely moving. "There's a very good one that meets weekly at Presbyterian. Many of my clients have found it helpful."

I wait for Julie to decline the offer, but instead I watch her nod her head.

Dr. Przybylinski recommends that our next step should be IUI—intrauterine insemination. "A very simple process. And only three hundred dollars or so an attempt. It's the last method so inexpensive, though, I'm afraid. But we don't have to cross that bridge just yet, eh?"

"Maybe we never will," Julie says, straining to smile.

"Exactly," I say, not wanting to seem uninvolved in the discussion.

Dr. Przybylinski proceeds as if he hasn't heard us. "It merely involves threading a very thin catheter through the cervix and injecting washed sperm directly into the uterus," he says, mimicking the procedure with his pincer-like fingers. "Virtually painless, and it takes all of about two minutes."

On our way out to the parking garage, Julie grabs me around the waist and says, "Well, I guess we've reached the point now where you might get me pregnant without ever having to touch me."

Or not, I think, unlocking the car. And it's at this moment, just as I'm imagining the true possibility of failure for the first time, that my desire to become a father flares within me more brightly than I've ever felt it. My heart stutters.

"Or not," she says, as if she heard my thoughts.

"How many of you newbies here tonight have found that most people don't really understand what you're going through?" This question is asked by Carrie, the smiling coordinator of the support group we've joined in North Dallas, a part of the city that we both typically find too snooty.

"You've got that right," grumbles a woman on the other side of the room, which brings laughs from several people.

Carrie then lets everyone know that, thanks to IVF—"in vitro fertilization, for those of you not far enough along to be hip to the lingo"—she has two beautiful daughters, Hailey and Hannah. Spreading her arms, Carrie says, "We're here to foster positive feelings and inspire hope in each other on our journeys toward parenthood."

The man next to me leans over and whispers, "I don't know about you, but this is the point where I could use a drink."

I chuckle, pretending to concur, but not loud enough to

draw the attention of Julie, who's listening attentively.

After half an hour of more affirmative talk, we break for ten minutes, but not before Carrie announces to us first-timers that the men and women typically congregate separately out in the hall at this point. "After all," she says, "as much as we'd like to think that our spouse understands every little thing we're going through, there's still something to be said for what women know about being women and men men, don't you think?"

By the snack machines, the man who was sitting next to me rests a hand on my arm and says, "I know what you're thinking. My wife and I are going on three years of this business." He holds up three fingers, then twists his hand around slowly in front of his face, as if only just now really grasping the amount of time that has passed. "My name's Clark, by the way."

"Phil," I reply, even though I've already introduced myself as Philip to the group, mainly because Julie still refuses to call me anything else.

"Some of us"—Clark gestures toward a few guys leaning against the wall, most of whom are texting on their phones—"like to tip a few back on Thursdays over at Beers 'n' Steers right off Northwest Highway, if you're interested. Some of the regulars aren't here tonight, but they never miss Thursdays." He winks. "We've convinced the wives that it's therapeutic male bonding. You interested?"

But before I can answer, Carrie shouts that time's up while windmilling her arms in the direction of our room, where we return to talk about embryo freezing until ten.

Everywhere we go now, I see babies. Babies in the parking lots, babies at the mall, babies in the elevator of Dr. Przybylinski's building. It doesn't particularly bother me—I still assume that *eventually* we'll have a baby—but I sense what it does to Julie, though she never says anything as we pass them sleeping in strollers or strapped to the chest of a parent, staring forward like a ship's tiny, proud figurehead. I see how her head turns, how her eyes linger.

And then there are the pregnant women. I never really paid much attention to them before, but now when I see them—dozens a day, it seems—their swollen bellies like watermelons begging to be thumped, I often find myself staring. Is it weird to find them sexy? Even when they seem to be in all sorts of discomfort as they wobble past, stiff-legged and splayfooted, their faces glisten in a way that seems almost spiritual. Even the ugly ones—the ones that make me wonder about the guys who put them in such a condition in the first place—I find almost beautiful as they shuffle along, massaging themselves absentmindedly.

What will Julie look like when it finally happens? I contemplate this while we eat fried rice at The Galleria's food court. Will her breasts grow to the size of Holly's?

"If the IUI doesn't work," Julie says, continuing where she left off right before we placed our order at the Golden Wok, "I'm thinking we should seriously look into adoption."

Before I can respond, she continues, saying again what I've heard her say several times before. "I mean, IVF is somewhere between ten and fifteen thousand a pop. And even that's still a crapshoot. According to his stats, Dr. P's success rate is around fifty percent or so. And that's *good.* Lots of doctors' rates are below that." She puts down her fork and massages her temples. "Plus there are all those goddamned injections I'll have to give myself. I just don't know."

Long before we even started trying to get pregnant we discussed adoption, how it really is the best thing to do considering how many unwanted children there are in the world. At the time I liked the idea of it, how it would make me feel good about myself for doing the unselfish thing, making the planet a little bit of a better place. But now that the topic has become less theoretical and more possible, I know I don't want to adopt. I like the thought of all that is in me, both good and bad, flowing out and reconstituting itself anew. With a clean slate, as it were. Besides, I'm not sure whether I could even love a child not mine by blood, no matter how awful I know that sounds. I imagine gazing upon a son or daughter from Guatemala or China or Russia, and never being able to extinguish the voice in my head whispering, *You're not really mine . . .*

"Adoption's expensive, too, you know," I say, repeating my same line from our previous conversations. "But like Dr. P said"—I drop my voice to a low, robotic monotone—"we don't have to cross that bridge just yet, eh?"

Julie laughs. Only now do I realize how long it's been since I last heard her do that.

"You know that's why I haven't divorced you yet, right? You still make me laugh, even when I'm feeling like shit."

Though I sense a subtext of criticism in the compliment, I try to ignore it, and, still in character, say, "Are you now ready to assist Mr. Fairweather in purchasing some new khakis?"

Her smile fades slightly. "Okay, funny man, don't overdo it."

Watching Dr. Przybylinski flexing his latex fingers as he steps between Julie's stirruped legs, I feel out of place, but then Julie takes my hand and pulls me closer to her side. The doctor's impassive face sinks from view below the tent of blue sheeting slung over her raised knees.

"This should feel no worse than getting a pap smear," he says, his voice slightly muffled.

I bend down and whisper, "Do those hurt?"

She holds a finger to her lips. "Shhhh."

I listen for a sound, maybe a soft squelch, but hear nothing. A man whose first name I don't even know is squirting my semen into Julie, and I'm standing here in shorts and tennis shoes, watching.

Half a minute later, Dr. Przybylinski's head rises into view again. "That's it. Now we wait. Just to be safe, I want you to lie here with your hips elevated for twenty minutes."

While I read articles to her from *Newsweek*, I wonder whether my little tadpoles are making their diligent way toward her expectant egg, or are they already floundering, already done for?

"I think you should go," Julie says.

It's a Thursday, which means that Clark and the other guys will be meeting up at Beers 'n' Steers. As far as I know, I'm the only one who hasn't shown up at least once so far. I've avoided it because I've never felt comfortable in bars—their atmosphere is too much like a locker room's, where a good time typically involves someone getting a swirlie or being lashed with a wet towel rolled into a rattail. Besides, no matter how screwed up I know most guys would think it is—no matter how odd even Julie probably thinks it is—given the choice, I prefer to spend my spare time at home with my wife. Plus, I don't particularly like to drink. And I certainly don't like being around people who drink as much as those who like bars typically do. Most of all, though, I don't want to go because I don't like how Clark and his North Dallas pals, so dapper in their expensive suits and monochrome ties, all look like former frat boys who are now attorneys and real estate developers. What can I, an ineffective sales manager for a company that sells cheap nutritional supplements, ever have in common with them, anyway?

"I have a pretty good time at Sweet Tooth with the girls," Julie says, now looking up from her book, which for once, I notice, doesn't concern either infertility or motherhood. "It might do you some good." The tone of her voice changes with this last statement. She seems to want me to hear something beneath her words.

"Am I in need of some good being done for me?" I ask, hearing an edge to my voice that I don't quite intend.

"You've been great through all of this, but I just think that, well, like Carrie says, men and women have different issues when it comes to this stuff." She closes her book and sets it in her lap, folding her hands over it. "I don't mean for this to sound critical, but sometimes I don't really get a sense of where you're at in regard to all this, so I'm thinking maybe you could use some time with guys going through the same thing, that's all."

"I'm in the same place you're at, Julie."

She reaches out and hangs her fingers from the front pocket of my shorts. "I know you are, hon. I know you are. But, see, for example, I don't even know what it's like for you at the Gladstone Clinic. Now with the couple of IUIs we've done, you've had to do it there something like four or five times, but you've never even said one word to me about it. Is it awful for you? Do you use porn? I don't even know."

I picture Holly's pubic hair, reduced to a neatly trimmed strip no wider than my pinkie finger. Sometimes when I close my eyes at night, I see her shaving herself with a foamy-headed razor. And then I remember my first sample, how humiliated I was to see that the lab technician extending a hand to receive my warm-bottomed cup was a woman—and not an ugly one, either. No, she was cruelly attractive, a green-eyed redhead with her hair braided in girlish pigtails.

"It's fine there," I say. "No big deal."

"And, believe me, I know how this has knocked things all out of whack." Her hand slides from my pocket to my crotch.

"Stop it, Jules." The subject makes me uncomfortable. Since starting the IUIs, we've only had sex a couple of times. No longer regularly driven to bed by duty, I hardly know how to approach her anymore. Now that we're depending entirely on a skillfully manipulated catheter to get her pregnant, when I think of sex I can only think of my pathetic sperm flailing and dying inside of her. It's simply easier not to complicate things; if nothing ever happens, if fertilization never occurs, I'd rather have only Dr. Przybylinski to blame.

She lets go of my pocket. "Humor me just this once."

"But it's called Beers 'n' Steers, for crying out loud. They'll probably string me up for not wearing boots and chaps. Besides, I humor you all the time, don't I?" It's starting to get dark outside now, so I turn on the lamp next to her. When I see the disappointed look in her eyes, it's too similar to the look I saw in them only a few days earlier, when she began spotting and thus knew that our most recent attempt at IUI had failed. "Okay," I say. "I'll go. For you."

On the way, I wonder about the things she shares at Sweet Tooth with those women she barely knows, the things she obviously doesn't feel comfortable sharing with me.

When I finally step into Beers 'n' Steers an hour late, having gotten lost after taking the wrong exit off Central Expressway and ending up in a scary part of Dallas entirely unknown to me, I try my best to look as though I instinctively understand how to conduct myself in a place like this, but no one even bothers to glance my way. Except for three male shadows bent over the bar, a woman dancing by herself in the yellow halo of the jukebox, and a stone-faced couple slouched at a dark table by the wall, the place looks empty.

"Look who's here!" shouts Clark, stepping around a corner, a longneck raised high. "Lord Philip has finally deemed us worthy of his esteemed presence."

Though I'm relieved to see Clark in jeans and a T-shirt, I'm embarrassed to hear that they think I've been avoiding them, so I try to come up with something that will make it clear that they have me wrong, but all I can think to say is, "Better late than never."

"Oh, I'm just fucking with you," Clark says, hanging his arm over my shoulders and leading me across the sawdusted floor toward a table beneath a bank of horned skulls.

Everyone at the table rises to shake my hand, their faces tomato red from the neon beer signs blazing on the opposite wall. It's strange to see all of them dressed just like Clark rather than in their usual attire; they look like a completely different group of guys. I, however, look as I always do. Julie calls it (affectionately, I think) my Sears-catalogue-boy look: plaid shorts, white polo shirt, and K-Swiss tennis shoes. As I grip each of their hands, I wonder which ones are to blame for their infertility woes. Any of them?

"Fresh Shiners all around," Clark calls to the waitress over the Johnny Cash playing from the jukebox. He pulls me down into the chair next to him.

"Usually we play pool in the back," says Charlie, who, with his sweat-damp hair and flushed face, looks as if he's been drinking twice as fast as the rest of the table. "But it seems the tables have been commandeered for the evening by some drugstore cowboys, so tonight we're just chillin'." He raises his bottle. "Just chillin' and swillin'."

"Don't mind him," Clark says. "He's just pissed off that they still haven't put Bob Wills on the jukebox like he keeps asking them to do."

"What self-respectin' Texas bar," Charlie shouts, to the amusement of everyone at the table, "doesn't at least—at the very fuckin' *least*—have 'Faded Love' on their goddamn jukebox is all I want to know."

"On top of being pissed off," Clark says, "he's loaded, too."

"For bear I am." Charlie raises an imaginary rifle and fires it at Clark.

The waitress sets a frost-whitened longneck in front of me, which I immediately raise to my mouth so as to appear happy and comfortable to be here. The intensity of the cold liquid shocks my teeth. After only a few swallows, I'm certain that I can already feel the alcohol swimming its way straight and deadly into my unaccustomed veins. It isn't a bad feeling at all.

Being the new guy, I naturally get asked questions, so I have to tell a bit about myself—where I grew up, where I live, what I do for a living. At first I'm self-conscious, fearing how they'll perceive me—the dull, unsuccessful guy living in the same dull suburb I've lived in all my life—but the beer helps. By the time I reach the bottom of the bottle, I nearly feel relaxed. The alcohol has worked through the muscles of my neck and shoulders, loosening them so much that only now do I realize how tight they were. And already my lips and tongue feel slightly tingly and rubbery, almost as if I'm having the same sort of allergic reaction that I get whenever I accidentally eat a strawberry.

"I didn't know it was even possible to live in Ivy that long without killing yourself," Trent says. "And I get to say that because I grew up there."

I would take offense at this except I remember that Trent's wife revealed at our last meeting that she's miscarried three times in four years.

With the arrival of the next round, everyone starts comparing stories about their REs. Clark and Trent go to a Dr. Malla, who apparently has a problem with body odor. Mitch and Graham go to a Dr. Seib, who they agree is almost too hot to take seriously.

"When she starts spouting all those medical terms," Graham says, "I just want to say, 'Look, I know for a fact that I could get *you* pregnant, so get your ass on over here.' You know what I'm saying?"

Only Charlie goes to Dr. Przybylinski. And just today, he and his wife found out that their first round of IVF failed.

"All that dough," Charlie says, pushing down an imaginary handle. "Down the shitter. Which is where I might as well have jerked off into, by the way."

I express my sympathy, but then in an effort to lighten the darkening mood, I stick my arms out stiffly in front of me and drone, "But I am king of all babymakers. Do not worry. I will make you pregnant. No big deal."

"Oh, man, that's so dead-on!" Charlie slaps the table, nearly spilling his beer, and looks around at the rest of the guys, his eyes shining. "That's *exactly* how the guy fucking talks, I swear!"

I struggle not to smile too broadly, delighted at the reaction, but I also feel a brief nudge of anguish, wishing that I'd given Beers 'n' Steers a chance long before.

When the third round appears, I guzzle what remains of my second bottle so that the waitress can take my empty along with the others. After I down half of the fresh bottle, savoring the numbness spreading its web a little further and deeper through my limbs, I decide that I'll take a cab home. And if Julie complains about it in the morning, I'll just remind her that I didn't want to come in the first place.

"Who here has to give the injections?" Clark asks.

Several of the guys roll their eyes and grunt.

"Lupron with Gonal-F?"

"Lupron with Gonal-F, baby!" Mitch raises his hand for a high-five.

"Please, no drug talk," Charlie shouts, waving his hands. "Please. At least no brand names. I don't want to hear them." He leans closer to me and says, "I'm a drug rep for Pfizer. And I guess it's safe to say I'm not exactly in love with my job."

"I hear you," I say, amazed at how quickly the camaraderie pulsing in waves around the table has come to include me.

"My wife fainted when she tried to do it herself," Graham says. "Fell out of the chair and busted her head wide open."

"My wife's gut swelled up like a whale's," Mitch says.

Despite knowing that IVF is probably our inevitable future, my attention fogs over as the discussion moves on to follicle stimulation and egg retrieval. Instead, I think about how nice it is just sitting here, boozy, temporarily disconnected from life's responsibilities, soaking up the smoke, music, and laughter. Except that I now realize I'm in fairly desperate need of emptying my bladder. Looking around, I try to determine where the restrooms might be, but there's nothing nearby other than reproductions of *Wanted* posters for Old West outlaws and rusted signs for Pearl and Lone Star Beer.

When I ask where it is, Charlie says, "I've gotta piss, too. Follow me."

Taking my newly acquired fourth bottle of Shiner with me, I unsteadily follow Charlie past the pool tables and down a hallway hung heavy with lariats, rifles, and spurs. This, I say to myself, enjoying the muddiness of my senses as I concentrate on not grazing the wall or weaving too conspicuously, *this* might be what it's really all about: just hanging out with the guys and drinking beer in a honky-tonk with nothing but Johnny Cash playing on the jukebox. I do wish, however, that I were wearing a pair of boots like Charlie's, which look so lived-in and used, instead of my stupid tennis shoes.

Up ahead of Charlie, who's whistling along enthusiastically to "Ring of Fire," I see the doors to the restrooms: one is marked *Steers*, the other *Heifers*.

Charlie stops and turns toward me. "Let me tell you, I still don't like having to take a piss in a place where they refer to us as steers."

"Why's that?" I ask, expecting a joke.

"Steers are bulls that've been castrated. It should be *Bulls*, not *Steers*." He shakes his head with a disgusted look on his face. "I understand how the dumb Yankees who probably own this place want to keep their cute little theme going, but at least they could do us the courtesy of getting *this* right." He starts to push through the door, but then stops. "Needless to say, if it was up to me we'd meet up somewhere else, but Clark's the boss. At least until he finally gets himself a kid."

Now he pushes through the door, and I follow him, stepping from smoky darkness into bright fluorescent light. To the left are two stalls—one out of order, the other occupied by someone wearing silver-tipped black boots—and to the right, instead of urinals there's an enormous tub, a thigh-high trough running the length of the wall. Immediately I want to turn and leave, push back through the door with an exaggerated look on my face that would make it clear to anyone watching that I wasn't looking for the restroom at all, that I walked through the wrong door entirely, but I can't, not while I'm with Charlie, who's still cheerfully whistling, already stepping between the two guys standing there—one a shrunken old man in a brown Western-cut suit, the other a hulking cowboy in stiff, blue-black Wranglers, a dizzyingly bright red- and turquoise-striped shirt, and a pristine, cream-colored Stetson.

With my pulse thrashing fitfully, I step to the other side of the cowboy. After setting my beer between my feet, my head dizzy from the sudden dropping and rising, I unzip my shorts. As I guide my tentative penis out into the chilly air, I close my eyes and order myself to relax, to relax. Willing myself to forget about the boy-sized man that the cowboy would see if he happens to look over, I pray that the appropriate muscles will cooperate, allowing my bladder to empty itself, and me to leave as quickly as possible. Despite the rank smell, I fill my lungs to their capacity and then exhale slowly through my nose, which feels oddly numb as the air rushes from it, as if it's no longer quite a part of my face. Swaying slightly, I try to imagine that I'm safe in the privacy of my own bathroom, so nicely scented by Julie's bowls of seashell-shaped soaps and potpourri, and I concentrate on the only sounds to be heard: the splash of piss, the occasional grunts and boot-scuffing of the guy in the stall, and Charlie's whistling, which continues unabated despite the muffling effect of the restroom door on Johnny Cash's sonorous voice.

To my surprise, within just a few seconds, my queasy insides calm, my taut muscles sag, and I feel myself let loose with a stream so steady and strong that I nearly smile when I open my eyes to watch what remains of my Shiners flowing out in a clear arc and splashing against the rusted bottom of the tub.

"Enough already, you fucking canary."

I know immediately that I'm not the one the cowboy is talking to, it's Charlie, but my stream still vanishes without even a dribble, shut off like a light switch by the alarm that sparks through me.

Charlie stops whistling long enough to say, "Hey, it's a free country, pal," and then resumes just as loudly as before.

Even though my bladder is still half-full, I zip up and turn away from the trough, knowing already that Charlie should have just done the easy thing and stopped. I want to leave, but I can't, at least not until it's clear that nothing more will happen. One after another, the old man, Charlie, and then the cowboy finish up right after me. The old man, adjusting himself as he walks, pushes through the door without looking in anyone's direction. For a moment, Johnny Cash's voice swells, but then the door shuts again. Moving past me without a glance, Charlie walks to the sink and begins washing his hands, still whistling. I don't like how his face looks; it's flat-eyed, waxen, shiny. In the bathroom's harsh light, he seems even more drunk than he did in the bar's red neon.

The cowboy steps up behind Charlie. "You don't seem to have heard me. I said, 'Enough already.'"

"Listen, my friend," Charlie says into the mirror, "since I was in no mood tonight to hear any of that Brooks & Dunn horseshit that you probably like, I punched ten dollars' worth of the Man in Black into that shitty-ass jukebox, and by God, I'll whistle along with him if I damn well please."

On the other side of the bathroom door, "Ring of Fire" fades away. The only sound now is the water splashing in the sink. I hope desperately that this was the last of Charlie's songs, but then there's Johnny Cash's deep voice again, singing, "Well, my daddy left home when I was three," and now, instead of whistling, Charlie begins to sing along: "and he didn't leave much for ma and me—"

In one motion, the cowboy grabs Charlie by the back of the collar and swings him around. "I told you to shut the fuck up already!"

Charlie, his face twisting fiercely, pushes back hard against the cowboy. "Get off me, you fucking wannabe!"

In shock at Charlie's fearlessness, I move closer, unsure what to do. In what seems like time slowed down by my drunkenness, I watch the cowboy cock his fist. Later, I'll wonder if I would've done anything if it hadn't been for the beer, but now, just as I hear Johnny Cash's voice bloom once again (someone must be coming in), I reach for the threatening arm, feel its strength straining against my fingers, see the man's Stetsoned head turn toward me, a look of confusion blurring the rage in his eyes . . . and then, without seeing anything else but light followed by streaking colors, I feel the left side of my face explode, followed by the back of my head cracking against . . .

When I open my eyes, Charlie and the cowboy are above me,

wrestling . . . dancing . . . then suddenly there are several more people around, yanking and tugging, yelling and cussing . . .

When I open my eyes again, I sit up despite the throbbing pain, and I watch two men leading the cowboy out, their arms laced across his back. His hat hangs dejectedly from one of his hands. Above his clenched, red face, the bald dome of his head glows as whitely in the light as his hat did. He's bleeding slightly from his mouth, and there are thin, dark smears on the turquoise stripes of his shirt.

Charlie is beside me now, laughing, helping me to my feet. "Holy shit, Phil. What the fuck was that, huh?"

I delicately touch the back of my head. A raw lump is rising under the skin. In the mirror, I press my fingers against the places where my face throbs; a purpling bulge is already distending from my left eyelid to the middle of my cheek. My eye seems to be sinking beneath the surface of my face as I watch. Tomorrow I know it will hurt like hell, but right now I kind of like the look of it, I have to admit. I've never had a black eye before, and though I've lived for years and years in constant fear of being challenged to one, I've never been in any kind of a fight before, either. But now I have been.

"Here you go," Charlie says, handing me my Shiner, which I now remember having set between my feet upon stepping up to the trough. "Where do those clowns get fucking shirts like that, anyway? He needed to get his ass kicked for that alone."

"Were you the one who bloodied him?"

"Not as much as I would have liked, but yeah. It wasn't like I could stand around doing nothing after he laid you out like that, right?"

A sense of gratitude comes over me like I've almost never known. It threatens to overwhelm me. I splash cold water on my face.

When we get back to the table, everyone rises up in shock at the sight of me.

"What the hell?" Clark shouts.

Once we sit down, Charlie recounts what happened. Even though only a few minutes have passed, I already feel that this is going to become one of those stories passed on by everyone at the table, possibly for years to come.

"You should've seen this guy," Charlie says, pulling me toward him. "He flew at that crazy motherfucker like nobody's business." Sweating and smiling, he bends his head over the fresh Shiner handed to him. "Saved my stupid ass from a haymaker."

Clark raises his bottle, shaking his head in awe. "Here's to Phil, then."

"Here's to Phil," everyone echoes.

I extend my beer to allow everyone to clink his bottle against mine. Then everyone drinks, including me. I feel . . . expansive, as if I could hug every last one of them. When a new bottle is brought to me, I stand, which makes the lump on my head throb even worse, but I ignore it. To keep from wobbling, I press my thighs against the table. Charlie, Clark, Trent, Graham, and Mitch all look up at me. I have their full attention. Johnny Cash is still singing—he's telling someone not to take his guns to town. A warmness like love floods through my body, even through my face, where I can feel my cheek ballooning toward my eyebrow, sealing off my sight.

"Here's to success for all of us," I say solemnly.

Everyone raises his bottle toward mine. "Here's to success."

"And here's to our wives," I say.

"Here's to our wives," the men echo, their upturned faces attentive and serious.

"And here's to our future children," I say quietly, in almost a whisper. The joyful heat in me intensifies, so much so that I can feel sweat trickling down my spine, wetting my shirt. Big, slow waves throb out from me with every heartbeat, flowing over everyone. I down as much of my bottle as I can manage in one long, voracious gulp. Beer dribbles down my chin, down my neck, but I don't bother wiping it away. When I lower the bottle to the table, I look down at my friends looking up at me. They know I'm ready. They know what I'm going to do. They know I'm taking a cab home and getting Julie pregnant with the biggest baby anyone has ever seen on the face of this earth.

The Leaves, They Pirouette

When ladies at the church ask you what you do—what you *are*—you say, "I'm a leaf blower," and you're happy saying this. You're happy being a leaf blower.

You're proud of your blower. It's an Echo PB-650. Your mother bought it for you. You've memorized everything about it: it has a 63.3 cc engine and a maximum blowing power of 205 miles per hour. It feels like a lion on your back, like a tornado. These are the things that come to mind when you think about how it feels—so warm, so powerful. Your old Husqvarna 165BT only had a 59 cc engine and a maximum blowing power of 190 miles per hour. You used to think your Husqvarna was the greatest ever. Now you realize that you might as well have been using a Makita. Or a Dolmar. Or even a Maruyama. Thinking about this makes you smile. No one knows leaf blowers like you. You get all the catalogues. They sit in a big stack beside your bed.

You love how beautiful your Echo is. You like how it's black and gray, not too-bright red like your old Husqvarna was. You wear black so that your blower almost looks like a part of you. Its wand is like your third arm.

You work alone. You're a freelancer. That's what your mother says you are. My little freelancer. You like this word. *Freelancer.* It makes you think of a knight riding his horse across the world in search of princesses to save and bad guys to fight. You wave your wand, and the bad guys run away, scared of your power. Whoosh, you say.

You have to go home whenever your Echo runs out of gas, and your mother fills it up. When you go out again, you feel brand new. The gas sloshes around heavily in its tank, and you know that there's no job too big for you now. You could go forever.

When you're out working, you like to listen to the music your mother put on your black iPod. You have to turn it up loud to hear it over your Echo. The songs don't have words, but you know what they're about because your mother told you their names. One is called "Autumn Leaves." One is called "Autumn in New York." One is called "Autumn Serenade." One is called "Falling Leaves." Your favorite, though, is just called "Autumn." It's only a piano playing. It sounds exactly like leaves would sound if they made music as they fell. Plink. Plink, plink.

You know that "autumn" and "fall" mean the same thing, but you like "autumn" better than "fall." It makes the leaves sound prettier. You wait all year for autumn. Autumn is like Christmas except there's no Santa for autumn. Dead leaves tumble and float with every gust of wind. The ground crunches beneath your feet, and the air smells like smoke. Autumn is better than Christmas.

Sometimes you get to burn the leaves. At home in the backyard, that is. You stand as close to the fire as your mother will let you, and you feel the smoke swallow you up. She tells you that outside fires like this are against the law, but then she says that she doesn't care. You love the way the smell gets in your clothes, your hair, your skin. At night, when you take a bath, you hold your clothes up to your nose and breathe in the smell until your head feels like a balloon.

You think about the days before leaf blowers. You remember them, but only just barely. You were a little boy. Your mother would get her rake out of the shed and make a big pile of leaves for you in the backyard. You'd run and jump right in the middle of it and wriggle yourself down as deep as you could until the light disappeared. You'd breathe in the smell of the leaves, close your eyes, and wish that this was what the whole world was.

You like cottonwood trees, because their leaves are as big as your face. You can poke eyeholes in them and use them as masks. When the wind blows hard, they skitter alive down the street, making clicking sounds like big, crunchy bugs. And you like every kind of oak tree, but particularly post oaks because their leaves are shaped like the big cross that hangs over your mother's bed.

You are a shepherd and the leaves are your flock. This is what your mother says to you. And Jesus is *our* shepherd. We are *his* leaves. When she says this, you see Jesus standing in the clouds with a shiny Echo on his back, blowing all the people around below him, separating into piles the sinners and the saved. Behind his flowing beard, he's smiling.

You like mulberry trees because their leaves are shaped like hearts, and you like maple trees because they turn the prettiest colors. They think they live in New England instead of Texas.

You've seen pictures of New England. Its leaves in autumn are beautiful. The leaves in Texas turn yellow sometimes, but mainly they just turn brown. When you're lucky, they turn orange or red, but that's rare. Still, you tell yourself, brown leaves need to be blown from one place to another just the same as orange and red leaves. It's not the leaves' fault that they're brown instead of orange or red. You feel sorry for the brown leaves when you think about this. They probably feel bad when they see the pretty leaves.

You get mad when you see big black bags full of leaves sitting on the curb, waiting to be picked up by the trashmen. It's wrong. Your mother tells you that not everyone likes leaves as much as you do. You don't tell her that, when no one's looking, you rip open the bags and free the leaves. You blow them around until it's as if they'd never been bagged ever.

You hear what people sometimes call you and say about you, but you pretend you don't. Your mother tells you that these people are evil sinners. They're like the man who threw that empty beer can at you that time, she says. And your father, because he left. They'll all go to Hell, she says, all those men, and you picture Hell with its fires and flames and you wonder whether the smoke smells sweet, like burning leaves.

You like when you're called Mr. Leafie. That's what some of the kids in the neighborhood call you whenever they see you blowing Bonham Street clean. Hey, Mr. Leafie! they yell. Hey, Mr. Leafie! You aim your wand at them, pretending that you're going to blow them away.

You keep a scrapbook of leaves that you like to look at during the winter when the trees and streets are sad and empty and there are hardly any leaves anywhere to be blown from one place to another. You picked some of the leaves because of their funny shapes. Some of the leaves you picked because of their interesting colors. You picked some of the leaves because they're perfect.

You have to quit when it gets dark. Once, you didn't quit when it got dark, and your mother came after you. She was mad. So now you always quit right when it gets dark and you walk home. You take off your Echo and set it in the corner of your bedroom. No one can touch it, not even your mother. You get in bed and look at the pictures in your catalogues or your scrapbook until you fall asleep.

At night, sometimes you dream that everyone is gone but you. Your mother is gone, too. While you look for her, the leaves rise up in front of your Echo like a snake with green, brown, yellow, orange, and red stripes. The snake winds through the air, plucking every last leaf from every tree, then rises straight up into the sky for miles until it reaches the moon. It makes you happy to watch the leaves spinning around the moon, but when you wake up, you're scared, like you were that time when your mother told you how one day she would leave for Heaven and you would have to go to a place where people might not need their leaves to be blown from one place to another. You hurry to the window to make sure that all the leaves are still there. There they are, just like yesterday. You rush to eat your breakfast as fast as you can. Your mother tells you to slow down, and you do, but you still eat as fast as you can, and then you hurry out with your Echo blazing. The leaves are happy to see you. You wave to them with your wand, and they dance for you.

Sub Rosa

Cody was listening for a distinctive sound: the thumping of boots against the worn, warped wood of Garrison Hall's floor. There it was, coming closer, steady as a metronome below the conversations bubbling around him. His fellow students all looked so at ease. Didn't they hear? Obviously they'd taken Dorrance for Latin III, not Witt, otherwise they'd know to quiet down. He considered warning the ones closest to him, but he didn't want to look like some goody-goody high-schooler, so he just watched, waiting to catch their reactions. A cute girl he recognized from Witt's class in the fall, Ms. Appleton, was looking around, too. She smiled conspiratorially when her eyes reached his; she obviously heard Witt coming, too. And even though he'd never even once spoken to her, he wondered if they might become confederates. Witt-veteran allies. He did his best to smile back, queasily excited at the thought of now having an excuse to approach her.

In truth, he didn't know why he liked Latin so much. Maybe it was because it made him feel smart to be studying something that everyone else thought only priests and monks cared about anymore. Or maybe it was because it was so straightforward and no-nonsense, unlike French, which seemed to make half the letters in each word silent for no apparent reason. Latin was just so . . . solid. That was it: it was exactly what he wasn't—tough, and so cocksure of its authority. Reeking of excess testosterone. It was a fist, whereas French was a flower. It was brutal, especially the way that Witt spit it at them as if he were Cicero himself, censuring Catiline. Or maybe it was simply because, for whatever reason,

Cody understood it—he *got* it.

"Tacete!"

Sentences died in mid-word, heads snapped forward. Witt, his trademark cigar unlit between his fingers, stood in the doorway. The air of the classroom still seemed to vibrate with the echo of his three-syllabled bark. Once all eyes were on him, he strode stiffly to his lectern and dropped his satchel to the floor with a book-heavy thud.

"Translation, please." His voice was now its usual deep, honeyed drawl. "If, that is, I could be heard about all that nattering."

Thankful that he knew, Cody raised his hand, but his hoped-for future friend had beaten him.

"Ms. Appleton." Witt pointed his cigar at her.

"'Silence,'" she said. "Or, more informally, 'Shut up.'"

Almost imperceptibly, Witt nodded. "Mr. Medford, since I also saw your hand, what else can you tell me about that word?"

Cody fought to keep his smile tamped down. "It's the present active imperative of the second conjugation verb *taceo, tacere.*"

"Singular or plural?"

"Plural."

"And why would that be?" Witt's pale, flat eyes stared at him.

"Because it was a command directed at more than one person."

Witt's face remained grim, though his voice lightened slightly as he tucked the cigar into the corner of his mouth. "How was your holiday, Mr. Medford?"

"It was wonderful, sir," Cody said, hoping that his face wouldn't divulge his lie; he'd done nothing but try to be of help to his mother, whose boyfriend of three years had broken up with her the day before Christmas Eve. "How was yours?"

"*Bene. Bene.* And you, Ms. Appleton?" he asked, though his

eyes didn't leave Cody. "How was yours?"

"*Bene*, Dr. Witt."

Only after he'd unloaded his stuff on that scorching August Saturday the year before, only after waving goodbye to his mother as she drove away, had Cody truly realized what had happened. He'd looked around at his new home, a furnished efficiency—its scratchy couch, dirty carpet, woodshop coffee table, and splitting kitchen linoleum—and wondered what he would make of himself here amongst so many thousands of other students. After two years at a community college, it was his chance at a fresh start in a new world.

Everything was exciting at first—decorating his place however he wished (posters of Monet's *Water Lilies* and Doisneau's black-and-white photograph of a couple kissing in Paris), sleeping and eating and watching television whenever and however long he wanted, going to the bathroom with the door open (though he only did this once, not being able to get over the feeling that somehow, someone was watching). But then classes started, and as he tried to blend in with all of the students happily shuffling down the Drag in their Ray-Bans, Corona T-shirts, and Greek-lettered shorts, his hopes for reinventing himself quickly began to wither. Here were people who belonged—they didn't feel sick to their stomachs or need a map to find their classes or fear being humiliated by professors amazed at their stupidity—and then here *he* was, dumb enough to have thought he could become one of them just by wishing it so.

By the third week of September he'd given up, though he continued to put up a good preppy front—khakis, starched oxford shirts, cordovan penny loafers—no matter how hollow he felt on the inside. So, carefully combed and freshly shaved but lonely and dejected, he sunk himself into Latin—datives of purpose, genitives of the whole, ablatives of separation.

After Witt dismissed the class, Cody, still flushed with pride from his successful conjugation, hung back so that he could surreptitiously fall in line alongside Ms. Appleton as everyone filed out. Watching her approach, he realized he'd forgotten how tall she was. She looked as if she might play basketball or volleyball, but he found it hard to believe that any of the university athletes would ever take a class as rigorous as Latin. He hoped that she would say something.

"Well, Mr. Medford," she said, "I guess the rest of our class chickened out and took Dorrance."

"I would have, too," Cody lied, "but I couldn't because of my schedule."

"Oh, come on, admit it. You love Witt. God knows I do. I mean, what's not to love? He's beautiful—like a young Paul Newman, except with a sexy, shaved head. I'm still no fan of that cigar, though."

"Okay, I love him," Cody said, his confidence swelling from her playfulness. "I have a painting of him above my bed. He's wearing nothing but a centurion's helmet."

She snorted. "See?"

"And he's brandishing a spear and yelling at me: '*Adsulta*, Mr. Medford, *Adsulta*!'"

"Perfect." They pushed through the doors of Garrison, out into the cold January morning. "I'm Vivian, by the way, not Ms. Appleton." She held out her hand.

"Hi, Vivian, I'm Cody." When he took her hand in his own, she pumped it once, then let go.

"Well, see you soon," she said, waving as she walked away.

"See you, Vivian," he called back, enjoying the chance to say her name again. While he watched her, the ghost of her hand in his slowly drifted away.

That first year, except to go to class, the grocery store, and the laundromat, Cody had rarely left his apartment. While listening to his neighbors partying, having sex, and coming home late and loud from the bars and clubs down on Sixth Street, he'd studied for tests, vacuumed the thin carpet, wrote essays, ironed his clothes, and watched television. But mostly he worked on his Latin, which meant memorizing: personal endings for the four conjugations, cases for the five declensions, present indicatives and future imperatives, jussive noun clauses, and pages and pages of vocabulary. And when necessary, he gladly sacrificed his responsibilities in other classes in order to guarantee that he'd impress with his faultless translations of passages assigned from Pliny and Terence.

After Latin I and II, with the same distracted graduate teaching assistant for both, it came time for Latin III. As if he were merely taking a break from digging fence-post holes on some dusty cattle ranch, Dr. Witt had come to class that first day in Wranglers faded pale at the seams, a white button-down with the sleeves rolled in tight folds past his elbows, and cowboy boots that he flaked clumps of dirt from the bottoms of with the blade of a wicked-looking pocketknife that he kept folded in a pocket of his jeans. Without first taking attendance or even introducing himself, he'd leaned back in his creaky chair and kicked his boots onto his desk.

"If you want to do well in this course, you'll have to do exactly what I ask you to do," he finally said, in a slow, deep voice that corresponded with his appearance but not with the photographs of Roman ruins behind him. "If you don't, you'll fail. I'll still be here next year no matter what, so I don't really care whether you do well or not, to be perfectly honest. For *your* sake, though, I hope that whomever you had for I and II prepared you for what I'm going to do to you." He pulled the first of that semester's many cigars from his shirt pocket and sniffed it. "You see, all I care about is Latin. And that it's done justice."

At this point he proceeded to explain the importance of Latin to the linguistic and cultural evolution of the Western world, but Cody hardly heard anything. Though his eyes never strayed from the cigar clenched like an aggravating bit between Witt's teeth as he talked, Cody kept hearing the man's earlier words.

What arrogance! Who did this Witt think he was, anyway? And yet Cody admired him, too, how intimidating he was. Authority emanated from him like heat. What would it be like to impress such a man, to do well for such a man?

Oblivious to the students muttering and cursing around him, Cody left the classroom as if under a spell, determined to make himself stand out.

Near the end of that first semester with Witt, Cody, upon receiving a quiz back that he'd passed with an A, saw a sentence scrawled beneath his grade: *See me this afternoon during office hours.* Immediately he felt ill. What was wrong? Did Witt think he'd cheated?

Later that day, Cody anxiously climbed to the top of Garrison where the offices of the classics professors were. The hall was vacant, quiet. It smelled of heated air and old books. He scanned the unfamiliar names on the closed doors that he passed, most of which were papered with conference posters, museum postcards, or yellowed cartoons clipped from *The New Yorker.* When he finally came to Witt's door, he found it bare except for a crude drawing of the Capitoline wolf suckling Romulus and Remus. Before knocking, he wiped his damp palms on his corduroys.

"Come on in."

Cody turned the knob and pushed the heavy door inward.

Witt was standing by an open window that looked out onto the cold, empty South Mall. He was smoking a cigar. "Take a load off, Cody. And shut the door. That bitch Boulter will make my life hell if she catches a whiff of me smoking in here again."

Though startled first by the informality and then the coarseness of Witt's language—he didn't even know who Boulter was—Cody appreciated being included in such a personal matter. He lowered himself into one of the two chairs positioned in front of Witt's massive, scarred desk. "I promise I won't tell anyone," he said, hoping to sound relaxed, which he wasn't at all.

Witt took a seat. With smoke leaking from his mouth, he said, "I'd be pretty disappointed in you if you did, I have to say."

Not knowing how to respond, Cody looked around the office while he waited for Witt to say more. On the walls not obscured by book-choked shelves hung framed prints of colorful Roman mosaics—furious gods, austere patricians in their robes, naked wrestlers grappling violently with each other. Behind Witt, on the only shelf free of books, sat miniature busts of Julius Caesar, Augustus, Hadrian, and Marcus Aurelius, all of whom Cody felt were glaring discontentedly down on him.

"You didn't think I called you here for something bad, did you?"

Feeling both relieved and sheepish now, Cody shrugged. "I have to admit I was a bit worried."

"A conscientious student should always be worried, if you ask me." He drew intently on his cigar and then asked Cody about his plans for the future. "You're graduating next semester, are you not?"

Cody nodded, but then he felt himself blush with shame at what he then had to confess, which was that he was moving back home with his mother until he figured out what to do next.

"Have you thought about going on to grad school?"

"I'm barely going to get out of here with my bachelor's," he said, exaggerating slightly. "I'm not exactly doing as well in my psych courses as I am in your class."

"Is that your major?" Witt scowled. "No, I'm talking about in *this*." He brought his hands down on a tattered copy of *Wheelock's Latin*.

"Seriously?" Cody felt the air around him change, as if it had grown thick and still. Graduate school? Latin? Him?

"Seriously, Cody. I'm talking Classical Languages and Literature." Witt stood. "If you want, we can talk more about it over at the faculty dining hall. I'm famished. Unless you're not interested, that is."

Cody felt honored that Witt thought so highly of him—*and*

he'd just invited him to dinner!—but *was* he interested? He didn't know. Nonetheless, he soon enough found himself walking across the Mall's expanse of dead November grass toward wherever the faculty lounge was, enveloped in the pungent fog of Witt's cigar.

"You went to *dinner* with him last semester?" Vivian's voice echoed in the silence of the library's third-floor quiet-study area. "Come on. You did not."

It was late February, and they were studying for the semester's first big test, the majority of which would involve translating a lengthy English passage into Latin, a task that, supposedly, no other Latin professor in the department ever required.

In five weeks, Cody had learned a lot about Vivian. For one thing, she didn't play basketball or volleyball for the university, though she had played in high school, at least until she messed up her knees. She'd almost majored in art history, but then she "woke up," as she put it, and switched to business administration ("Can you imagine? I mean, I love Johns and de Kooning, but come on!"). And now she already had a job lined up in Chicago for after graduation, even though she didn't intend to stay there for more than a year because, as she put it, she wanted her MBA "done with" before she got too used to being out of school and making "pretty good" money.

And she had a boyfriend, of course. A rugby player, no less. She went to see him play every Saturday morning.

"We've been together off and on for almost a year, but it's not like it's ever really been that serious. I mean, he's fun, but . . . I don't know. We run at the track a lot."

Cody had struggled to keep his face from betraying him upon hearing this because, by this time, he'd fallen for her. And it was, in fact, the word "fallen" that he heard in his head when he thought of her—her black hair always haphazardly gathered in a ponytail, her tiny nose that looked as if an invisible hand kept it slightly thumbed at the world. Reading on his apartment's skin-chafing couch, writing at its wobbly desk, stir-frying vegetables at its stove's only working burner, he heard: *I'm falling for her, I'm falling for her.* He told himself that he definitely wasn't stupid enough to be thinking in terms of love, but then he realized that having to tell himself this at all surely couldn't be a good sign, particularly when, even before learning of Kirk, he'd already accepted the impossibility of ever drawing her romantic attention. After all, what girl could possibly be interested in a guy who'd never be able to pick her up and carry her over the threshold, a guy who'd never be able to give her a kiss while they were standing unless he brought along a stepstool? Nevertheless, hearing about Kirk had still stung.

Cody ran his highlighter over a line that he'd written in his notebook: *Indirect command = ut (nē) + subjunctive.* "I did. I swear. We ate at the faculty dining hall right before Thanksgiving."

She wanted to know the reason for the invitation, of course, so he told her about Witt's suggestion and how he had then gone on to indicate a few ways that Cody might be able to get himself accepted without having an undergraduate degree in classics. "He said that so few people want to pursue advanced degrees in classics nowadays that departments will pretty much work with anybody who's interested. As long as they're not total idiots. And willing to take the necessary courses to catch up, of course."

Vivian pouted exaggeratedly. "How come he never took *me* to dinner to talk about that? No offense, but you're no smarter than *I* am in Latin. Plus I'm prettier." A corner of her frown rose into a crooked smile. "But only a little."

"Maybe I just seemed more recruitable."

"Not that I would've been interested," she continued. "I mean, can you imagine anything more impractical?"

"How come you're taking it, then, if it's so impractical?" Cody asked, feeling immediately protective of both Latin and Witt.

She shrugged. "Because I aced it at my stupid Catholic high school, and I wanted something I could count on to pad my GPA."

Despite the gorgeous smile on her face as she said this, Cody hated her a bit at this moment, because he knew that Latin—that everything, probably—came easier to her than it did to him. "Let's get back to it," he said, raising his notebook. And though he would have been happy to study all night just as long as she stayed there with him, he added, "I really don't want to be at this until dawn."

What he didn't tell Vivian about his dinner with Witt was how they had talked about other things, as well. Struck by how pleasant Witt seemed outside of class, Cody had found himself opening up when asked personal questions instead of doing what he typically did, which was either responding evasively or simply lying.

After patting his lips with a napkin that he then dropped onto his empty plate, Witt had said, "Cody, I'll be honest. You can tell me that it's none of my business, but looking out at you sitting there in my class, I can't help but get the sense that you're not all that happy a fellow, that maybe you've got issues you're dealing with. Am I correct in that assumption?"

A few seconds passed before Cody said anything—and these seconds were spent debating whether to put up the usual screen or to tell the truth—but when he eventually said, "You're right, I'm not happy," thus confessing his wretchedness out loud for the first time to anyone, he felt better than he had in a long while. "To be honest, I'm miserable."

Though Witt had to leave soon after this, he walked with Cody back across the Mall, which was now completely dark except for the smudged light cast by the lamps lining the sidewalks along its edges.

"I want you to know something," Witt said, turning toward him. "If you ever feel the need to talk, you should call me." He pulled a business card from his pocket and handed it to him. "My home number's on the back."

Embarrassed but appreciative, Cody took it. "Thanks, Dr. Witt."

"When we're not in class, you can call me Roy."

Cody had to force himself to say it: "Okay, Roy."

Witt rested his hand on Cody's shoulder. "Believe it or not, Cody, I haven't always been the well-adjusted amazement that you see before you now. I've had my own issues, too." He paused, seeming to be considering whether to say more. "At least you're from the city, though. You *are* a city boy, correct?"

"Well, a suburb."

"Of?"

"Oklahoma City."

"Good enough. Try growing up in Hockley County, Texas, where a place called Levelland was a metropolis, and Lubbock might as well've been Rome. To say that my daddy didn't know what to make of me would be a tremendous understatement. He *still* doesn't know what to make of me. Not until I escaped did I learn that I could live life on *my* terms." He lifted his hand from Cody's shoulder. "Anyway, enough of that. I'm headed this way now, so you take care."

Still feeling the warm, heavy weight of Witt's hand, Cody watched the man disappear into the fog. How wretched must I seem, Cody wondered, for someone so busy and brilliant to take the time and effort to reach out to me? Pretty wretched, he guessed. He raised the card to his nose to see if it smelled of cigar smoke. It did.

April arrived as a gray drizzle. In class, Witt continued to treat him no differently than he had the previous semester, before or after their dinner together. Looking him in the face, Cody still could see no evidence of the man who had touched his shoulder in the chilly darkness of the Mall four months earlier. Cody had never called, but he hadn't thrown the number away, either.

He had, however, visited Witt during office hours a few times. Each time he'd come with a carefully chosen question—*is the dubitative subjunctive just a different name for the deliberative subjunctive?*—but really, he just liked sitting there amidst the books and the heads of emperors, listening to Witt, who usually dispatched his question within only a few seconds and then went on from there to discuss at length something tangential brought to mind by his answer, whether it be Cicero's rhetorical tactics or the gossipy fun of reading Suetonius's *De Vita Caesarum*. Neither he nor Witt ever mentioned again the personal nature of their first conversation, but Cody could always tell by the way that Witt looked at him as he asked how he was doing that it was more than just perfunctory small talk. Though he appreciated this, Cody never said anything other than "Fine," no matter how dreadful he felt, though just sensing that someone such as Witt cared about him made him feel better, especially whenever their discussion made its way back to the topic of graduate school.

"What about Vivian?" Cody asked once, curious. "You know, Ms. Appleton? How do you think she'd do in graduate school?"

Witt shook his head dismissively. "She's smart, but she's not as serious about Latin as you are. You understand the importance of keeping it alive. Especially in this dim age." He drew deeply on his cigar. "Besides, I'm pretty sure she's only interested in getting her MRS degree."

"Actually, I think her major's business administration."

Witt smirked as he flicked his cigar over a coffee-stained saucer. "I mean that she's one of those gals whose main goal in college is to find a husband, to become a Mrs. Don't let her kind fool you—they're not nearly as liberated as they'd have you think."

Understanding the joke now, Cody knew he should stick up for Vivian, but doing so might diminish Witt's opinion of him, and he couldn't bear that—it felt too good—so he just nodded in agreement.

By the time May arrived, spring had exploded. Along with the vegetation, students had burst forth from their winter sheaths. Vivian came to class in shorts that seemed to double the length of her already wonderfully long legs. Cody struggled to keep his eyes on Witt and the *Aeneid.*

"Nothing is off limits on next week's final," Witt said, not looking up from whatever book he had before him on his lectern. "And if you do poorly, even if you're carrying a solid A right now, you'll find yourself rowing up that famously shitty creek."

Vivian turned to Cody, her face contorted in exaggerated fear. "We'll have to prepare ourselves, won't we?"

"Absolutely."

Because the library would be overflowing with students desperately cramming, she suggested they get together at his apartment on the night before the final. "I'd say come over to my place," she added, "but my annoying roommates wouldn't let us get anything done."

As he readied his apartment for her visit, he had to keep reminding himself not to think of this as a date but as just another study session. Their last one.

When he finally heard her knock, he checked his reflection before opening the door to make sure that he didn't have anything in his nose or teeth. She stepped inside, bringing the warm fragrance of the May evening in with her.

"God, your place is so *clean*," she said, looking around. "You should see Kirk's. It's like I need a tetanus shot every time I go over."

"I guess I'm just sort of anal that way," he said, immediately regretting the explicitness of his word choice. "You know, a neat freak."

After pushing the rickety coffee table against the couch, they sat cross-legged next to each other on the floor, fanning their books and notes before them.

"Well," she said. "I guess this is it, huh?"

"Yeah, I guess so." And though he knew that she was referring to the end of Latin and the end of school, to him her words meant something different. He only hoped that he didn't look as sick as he felt.

Poring over everything that seemed like something that Witt

might sadistically enjoy throwing at them, they stayed on task for several hours, jacked up on freshly ground mocha java, but a few minutes before midnight, with their knees and backs aching, they finally agreed to take a break.

"I hope we're right about how Witt's thinking," Vivian said, making her way stiffly to the bathroom.

"Me, too," Cody said, but she'd already shut the door behind her. He stepped into his tiny kitchen to make more coffee.

For a few seconds he paused in his bean grinding to listen to the splash of her urine. Though he was ashamed of himself for eavesdropping on such a private moment, he thought about how, if they were a couple, it would be exactly like this: just two people doing normal things like grinding coffee beans and going to the bathroom. How wonderful that would be.

After they returned to their positions on the floor, despite their best efforts, they couldn't reclaim their focus on Aeneas and Turnus hacking away at each other. Though still staring at the Latin, Vivian started talking about other things—her other finals, how sick of studying she was, how sick of school she was, how excited she was about moving to Chicago.

"I hear you," Cody said, though all he could think of was how he wished he could prolong it all somehow.

A ragged, tired silence then settled between them. He watched her face grow serious and the focus of her eyes soften while her fingers absentmindedly traced the cover of her book. He could tell that she was thinking about something. Was she worrying about what Kirk would think of her studying alone in another guy's apartment? Or had she not told him, and now was feeling guilty? When Kirk found out, would he come after him, seething with suspicion and distrust, determined to give him a pummeling? As if on cue, an ambulance whirled by outside, its siren ululating.

When Vivian finally looked up, her cheeks were slightly flushed, as if she'd been holding her coffee cup too close to her face. "Did you know that Witt's gay?"

In the stillness, Cody's thoughts had slid from Kirk back to the bleakness of the year facing him: living under his mother's roof and doing nothing but working for yet another year in the bookstore on Francis Avenue. And applying to graduate school. At least he had that to look forward to. "Huh?" It took a moment for her words to settle into place, but when they did, he realized that she was just joking. "Come on."

"No, he is. Really. He told me when I went to talk to him yesterday."

Despite knowing that such a thing shouldn't matter to him, Cody felt a chill inch across his skin. Witt was gay? Hearing this was almost like the moment he'd found out from his mother that his father had been cheating on her for years. Witt, always standing so brazen in front of the class, planted rock steady in his boots and jeans and starched white shirt with the sleeves rolled up past his burly forearms, bellowing furiously at someone in the back row for pronouncing Cicero's name with a sibilant 'C'. . . . Gay?

"No way," he said.

"Tell me about it." Vivian laughed, but what came out was no more than a puff of air, a sigh. "I nearly cried. I mean, what a horrible waste. It just goes to show you, though. You never can tell. And I guess sometimes a cigar *isn't* just a cigar, you know?"

Cody was coming out of his haze of shock, but only slightly. "How did that even come up? I mean, how—"

"We were talking about you."

"Me? But—"

She looked up, into his eyes. "He asked me if you'd come out to me."

"Come out?" The phrase didn't immediately mean anything to him. *Come out?* But then he understood. The coffee in his stomach bubbled. "You mean like out of the closet?"

She nodded.

"Why would he even think that?" Anger flared inside him as if a hot wire had been threaded down a vein or artery, shocking his heart with an electrifying jolt.

Vivian shrugged. "He said he can just tell when someone is. Or when someone's unsure about it. He said he knows what it's like. 'To be there,' as he said. Where you're at."

"Where I'm at?" He yelled this, and he saw her flinch. His next question was quieter and calmer, but inside he was still yelling. "What did you tell him?"

"I told him no."

"No what? That I hadn't come out to you?" He was trying to keep his voice calm. "Is that all? Didn't you tell him that I'm not gay?"

She turned her face away from him. "No."

"Why not?"

She didn't answer immediately. When she did, she said, "Because I didn't know whether you were or not."

"What do you mean—"

"I mean I didn't know for sure, Cody." Her voice was now as loud as his. "I thought maybe you were. I mean, I couldn't tell." Her face reddened further. "Because it's not like you've ever made a move on me, you know, no matter how much I've ever flirted with you."

"Made a move? Vivian, you've got a boyfriend," Cody said, not liking the infuriated whine that he heard in his voice. "A boyfriend!" And what she called flirting? That was just her being friendly. He knew this even if she didn't. Because that was the sort of person she was. She'd *never* flirted with him. *No one* had. Ever!

"Come on, Cody. Please! You know I'm not serious about Kirk. You know it! Kirk is an idiot. He's just fun. We've got *nothing* in common. He's a kinesiology major, for Christ's sake. Besides, we hardly go out anymore."

As another ambulance shrieked past outside, all that had just been said continued to buzz and cry in Cody's head. To his disgust, he felt near tears. Keeping his eyes focused on the Latin notes sitting in his lap, he finally said, "Just because I'm not a fucking neanderthal doesn't mean that I'm gay, you know."

Silence swallowed his words. But then she said, "You should

see Kirk. Talk about a neanderthal. He's like six-four, two-thirty. He's even got a hairy back. And there's nothing he loves more than when he has to get stitches after a rugby match." Cody watched her shake her head as if in disbelief at what she'd just said, but why was she telling him this? Did she want to make him feel even worse? Was she even paying attention? "You see . . ." She stopped. "You see . . . it's only hulks like that who've ever asked me out. No one else ever wants to be seen with an amazon like me."

Hearing this, Cody became suddenly and acutely aware of his blood, how hot and thick it felt inside him. He knew what he wanted to say, and as he struggled to determine whether he could manage it, his sludgy pulse throbbed sickly.

Though his voice sounded so tiny in his ears that he wondered if she could even hear him, he finally said, "*I* would."

At the final, he felt as if all of his senses were vibrating at an imperceptibly high speed. His eyes, jittering, didn't even need to blink. With Vivian beside him (in one of his striped oxford shirts that was a size too large for him but just right for her) and Witt brushing past every few minutes, vigilantly stalking the aisles in search of cheaters, Cody watched his pencil taming the sentences writhing like asps in their futile efforts to evade him. He felt transcendent, herculean, as if he were reclining above the classroom on a floating divan. Even as his thoughts kept returning, again and again, to a single image from the night before—the elongated nakedness of Vivian's body stretched across the fresh sheets of his bed, looking exactly like one of Modigliani's beautiful reclining nudes that had glowed in the darkness of his art history class—the words effortlessly slipped into place.

By the time the first students began turning their tests in and leaving, their faces slack and pale, he was already finished, but he pretended not to be. He'd decided to stay until he was the last one left. Keeping his head bent over his desk as if he were diligently focused, or even struggling, he doodled in the margins of Witt's exam.

With twenty minutes to go, only four people were still working. Vivian was one of them. But then she gathered her things and stood.

"I'll be outside," she whispered close to his ear.

He nodded without looking up, not wanting her to see that he was done.

As if by arrangement, the remaining three finished simultaneously. Still without looking up, he listened to their steps and voices fade as they moved out of the room and down the hall.

And then it was quiet. He could feel Witt staring at him from his perch at the lectern.

"Time to hand it in now, Mr. Medford. *Tempus fugit*, especially when taking a final."

Cody set his pencil down and walked his test up to Witt, who slid it into his satchel. And just like that, Cody thought, college is over. Outside on the grass, beneath the leafy oaks, Vivian was waiting for him. They were going out to lunch. Greasy burgers and onion rings at Hut's. She couldn't believe that he'd never been there. *We have to go*, she'd said. And then he hoped that they'd go back to his apartment. To have sex again. And again. This time in less of a clumsy rush. This time with nothing to prove to anyone. He wanted to take his time, to savor it, to savor her. But as badly as he wanted to run out to her as fast as he could, to start their first full day together, he couldn't, not yet, not unless he wanted this to hang forever over his head.

"Just being cautious?" Witt asked, buckling his satchel and slinging it over his shoulder. "Or were you having genuine difficulty?"

Cody hardly even heard the question. Had the night with Vivian not happened, he would have slunk out without saying anything. But the night before *had* happened, and he no longer was who he once was. "You had no right to talk to Ms. Appleton about me."

Witt's weathered face softened slightly. He held his hands out in a gesture of supplication. "*Mea culpa*, Cody. I was just trying to help. I thought you might want it. Or need it, even if you never asked for it. I thought—"

"I'm not a homosexual."

Witt opened his mouth to say something, but he shut it again. Then he said, "That's great. I'm happy to hear that." He started toward the door at the back of the room. "Look, it's been great having—"

"I'm with Ms. Appleton now," Cody said. "We're together," he added, though he suddenly feared that he might be jinxing himself by saying so. "We're a couple."

"Hey, congratulations." Still walking, Witt nodded. "Good for you. She's a smart girl. And as I was trying to say just now before you so rudely interrupted me for a second time, I enjoyed having you in class this year."

Cody felt slightly faint as he watched Witt drawing nearer to the doorway. In just a matter of seconds it would be too late. He feared what he might hear, but he needed to know. "So . . . was all that grad-school talk for real? Or were you just hitting on me?"

For a moment Cody thought Witt was simply going to continue walking until he reached the door, ignoring the question entirely, but then he stopped, pivoted on his heel, and came back toward him, his swift steps thudding against the floorboards like falling stones. Not until he was only inches away did Witt stop.

With a finger that punctuated each word with a stiff thrust against Cody's chest, he spit, "Don't flatter yourself, my friend. You understand me?"

Surprised by Witt's sudden ferocity, Cody took a step backwards, unable to say anything.

Apparently satisfied, Witt turned away, but then he turned back, his finger stabbing at Cody again. "How *dare* you! Forget everything I *ever* said to you, do you understand me? Forget grad school, forget coming to me for a letter of recommendation. Or for anything else, for that matter, you ungrateful little piss-ant."

"Please, sir, wait," Cody finally called out, but he'd waited too long; the only response he received was the reverberation of his own voice and the receding tick-tock of boot heels as they ebbed down the hall, then up the stairs. Lightheaded, his heart clubbing against his breastbone, he took a seat in the empty first row, the momentary bravado awakened in him by Vivian now decimated. What, in his sex-mad, sleep-dead haze, had he done?

When he finally stepped out of Garrison Hall, Vivian smiled and waved at him. Just as he'd pictured her, she was sitting right outside, beneath one of the Mall's enormous trees.

"What took so long?" she asked as they started walking toward Hut's. "Was Witt taking one final stab at convincing you to follow in his footsteps?"

Not sure what sort of footsteps she was referring to, he took her hand and squeezed it.

She squeezed back. "His *Latin* footsteps, Cody." She laughed. "God, I swear."

Having not admitted to her his wish to pursue Latin further, he was safely able to laugh at this and say, "He did, but I told him to forget it."

Never did he confess to Vivian how much in those last few months of his senior year he had come to visualize himself going on to graduate school and becoming a scholar of Latin, making Witt proud of him. And never did he tell her what happened in Garrison 214 on that last day after everyone had left—not even much, much later, when it might have been something for them to laugh about together.

Neither did either of them ever bring up with the other the awkward conversation that had precipitated their first kiss (and then, swiftly, more) on that night before Witt's final. Not even once. It was as if they silently agreed to accept as truth the silly story they came to tell people who asked them, "How did you two end up together, anyway?" Though Cody knew what they were really asking—"How did *you* ever get a leggy wonder like *her*?"—Vivian always responded, "It just kind of happened when we were cramming for a final: he slipped something in my coffee, jumped my bones, and we've been together ever since." After hearing it enough, Cody nearly came to believe that it really had been like that on their first night together. It made for such a better memory than what he tried his best to forget, that even the woman who eventually became his wife had once had her doubts about him.

But most of the time, quite honestly, none of this mattered. It was history; it had no real bearing on their life together. He was happy. *They* were happy. He loved her, and he knew that she loved him, too, as difficult as that was for him to comprehend at times. Even after their wedding it still seemed just too good to be true, just too impossibly wonderful to be true. She was so smart, so beautiful (at least to him, and if no one else thought so, he didn't give a whit), so fantastic. Sometimes when he was feeling particularly unsure of himself, he would ask her what exactly it was that she saw in him, and when she'd respond with an extensive list of his fine qualities ("You're devoted, affectionate, considerate, sensitive . . .") while seductively dragging the tips of her fingernails across his scalp or down his back, he always felt better (how could he not?), agreeing that, okay, so maybe he did possess some of these qualities, but usually he couldn't help but then mention their height differential, which was extreme enough that he feared that, at least occasionally, when briefly glimpsed from the corner of someone's eye, he must get mistaken for her rather tall young son.

"My father is no taller than you," she said the first time he mentioned it, "and I worship my father—always have, even after I passed him in height in the seventh grade. So, unless you're looking to upset me, we should just drop it."

Nevertheless, despite his doubts and insecurities, he did eventually come to see their being together as natural. As inevitable. He hated the corniness of the phrase, but he believed that, truly, they were "made for each other."

Sometimes, though, especially when he knew that she was

watching him struggle desperately with something that no respectable husband should ever struggle with, like a flat tire or the twists and turns of a road map, he would wonder: "How uncertain of me was she back then, and does she ever get that way now?" After all, he thought, it wasn't as if it were so strange to hear about average-seeming men living furtive, unsavory lives behind the backs of their wives and children; it happened. When she saw the muscled arms of the male models in the perfumed pages of her fashion magazines, did she ever think fondly of Kirk, and what could have been? Did she ever wonder if, maybe, the scam of a lifetime had been pulled on her? Did she ever wonder if Witt had known something that her future husband had never revealed to her? Or worse: that Witt had known something that her future husband had never even acknowledged to himself as the truth?

And though he'd agreed that it was a great idea when she proposed that they include a phrase from Virgil's *Eclogues* at the bottom of their wedding invitations as a way of privately acknowledging their birth as a couple—*Omnia vincit amor et nos cedamus amori*, love conquers all; let us all yield to love—frankly, he couldn't stomach the sight of Latin anymore; it was like running across an embarrassing old photograph from high school, one that had caught him wearing a favorite shirt that, in retrospect, made him look utterly ridiculous. Of course, though, just as for Vivian, Latin certainly did bring to mind their good life together, as well—after all, if it hadn't been for Latin . . .

But no matter how hard he tried to keep his memories limited to her, he just couldn't do it. *Annus mirabilis, in loco parentis, persona non grata, ecce homo* . . . yes, these phrases did often bring back the delicious coffee flavor of her mouth, the miraculously slick heat of that very first moment when she'd enfolded him fully, but it also brought back memories of other things, like the crack of boots against wood floors, the stench of cigar smoke, the pain of a dime-sized bruise left on his chest by a jabbing finger. . . .

Horsehead Crossing

All the boy had been told was that they were driving to a place called Horsehead Crossing. Falling asleep in the backseat, he pictured hundreds of horses shaking their manes as they galloped over a bridge. When they woke him, saying, "We're here, sleepyhead," he squinted through the sun-shot window and saw nothing but white and brown and dirt and dust and heat. He stepped out of the car into a scorching light that poured through his skin. Behind the rest of his family, he stumbled over the loose rocks.

"The mighty Pecos," said his Uncle Darrell.

"The only place to cross it for miles and miles," said his Uncle Dwight.

"But they've put the marker in the wrong goddamn place," said his grandfather, who was extremely old and even nearer death than the boy imagined. "We drove our cattle across further on down."

Looking at the nothingness around them, the boy asked: "Where are the horses?"

Everyone hooted.

"They called it Horsehead Crossing because they used to hang horse skulls on the mesquite to warn people away from watering here," said his father.

"High saline content," said his Uncle Darrell. "The alkaline soil's to blame."

"This is part of your heritage," Uncle Dwight said to him. "You should feel a sense of pride when you see this place."

The boy squinted. The river looked dirty and sad, like

someone had forgotten to leave the faucet running.

"I want to go back to Granddaddy's house," he said.

What else the boy remembered seeing that day:

. . . a big, black mama scorpion with hundreds of baby scorpions on her back, all of them the sick, pale color of skin underneath a bandage left on too long. His uncle Darrell slipped off one of his boots, raised it high over his head, and slammed the heel down on them so hard that bits and pieces of the mama scorpion and her hundreds of babies and the rock beneath them flew into the air in a great explosion.

. . . his Uncle Dwight blowing the head off a rattlesnake with a shotgun.

. . . his uncle Darrell scraping scorpion guts from the heel of his boot with the blade of his pocketknife.

. . . his Uncle Dwight cutting the rattle free from the snake and then shaking it like a maraca up next to everyone's ear.

"Come on," says his wife twenty years later when he tells her of this day. "That sounds like just a bunch of Texas macho crap to me."

"I know it does, but it's the truth, I swear," the once-little boy says, though he's much less sure of the story's truth than all that. What he does know is that, lying in bed, still buzzing from red wine and pot and sex, the story feels good and bona fide as it slips from his mouth.

Annoyed and feeling suddenly untethered there in the middle of the wintry, rural darkness of the Pennsylvania Dutch country, he rolls away from his wife, who grew up in Minnesota and doesn't know shit about scorpions and rattlesnakes, and he lets himself ease into sleep while thinking of Uncle Darrell and Uncle Dwight and Granddaddy, all dead and gone for so long now.

It would be fitting to say that he dreams of horses, scorpions, and rattlesnakes, but he doesn't. Or, even better, it would be fitting to say that he dreams of what really happened on that day when he was a little boy, but he doesn't do that, either. Instead, he dreams of sleeping sticky and hot in the backseat of a car, listening through his dream's ear to Hank Williams singing on the radio about being so lonesome he could cry.

The New Father

The new father pushed his son's stroller along the quiet neighborhood's sidewalks every day that the weather allowed. Sometimes Daniel gurgled and cooed beneath the stroller's hood as Lawrence pushed him north up Travis, west all the way down Crockett, south down Bowie, and then east all the way up Fannin, which brought them back to their street, Bonham. Other times, though, his son began mewling and keening soon after leaving home, compelling Lawrence to wheel the stroller around before even reaching Travis. Still other times, Daniel made no noise whatsoever for blocks and blocks, having been lulled to sleep by the rhythm of the wheels rolling across the evenly spaced grooves in the sidewalk.

Occasionally, when there were no noises to be heard, those times when he didn't know for sure whether his son had faded into sleep or not, Lawrence worried as he pushed the stroller along. He knew it was silly to worry—Daniel was surely just fine there beneath the stroller's hood—nevertheless, he found himself worrying. He wouldn't, however, immediately allow himself to pull back the hood to check on his son, even though he couldn't keep himself from imagining Daniel lying there not breathing, his skin turning blue. He didn't want to be one of those parents who worried incessantly, convinced that his child was always on the verge of choking on a Cheerio, for instance, or dying quietly of SIDS while lying beneath the crib's still mobile in the quiet dark of the nursery. Then, having forced himself to push the stroller past several more houses, seeing nothing but an awful holographic image hovering before his eyes, Lawrence would quickly—but gently, so as not to wake Daniel if he were, after all, just sleeping—pull back the stroller's hood . . . and smile at the sight of his son breathing just fine, sucking away at his binky, staring up at him, seemingly having been waiting all this time for his father to look down upon him.

Regardless of how much he loved his baby son, sometimes Lawrence wished that he didn't have to be the one responsible for him, day in and day out. Sometimes he wished instead that he could be the one his son looked forward to seeing walk through the front door at the end of the day with his suit jacket slung over a shoulder and his tie loosened just so. But he would never be greeted by a running, smiling son, a son yelling, "Daddy! Daddy!" because he was the one always making dinner, washing the dishes, running the vacuum cleaner, doing the laundry, turning on *Sesame Street*, *Teletubbies*, and *Boobah*; because he was the one always changing his son's diapers, suctioning snot out of his nose with the blue bulb, fishing inappropriate stuff from his mouth, wiping away the crud that accumulated in the plump folds of his neck. No, because he was forever doing these sorts of things he would never be greeted with a running, smiling son, a son yelling, "Daddy! Daddy!"

But both he and Bethany had decided that, though not ideal, this was the most logical and appropriate route for them to take. Had *he* been the one earning more money, she would have happily stayed home. For the most part, she was good about not making him feel too guilty about this necessary arrangement, but sometimes he saw something in her eyes that she tried to keep hidden. It was a look that was one part anger, one part sadness, and he saw it anytime that she had to yield to his knowledge of any of Daniel's myriad idiosyncrasies and desires. When he calmed their son when she couldn't, he saw the look, faint though it was. When he suggested or warned her against a certain activity—"He doesn't really seem to like the rainbow bear anymore, hon"—he saw it. When he received a reaction from their son that she obviously had been hoping to receive herself, he saw it.

To ease her mind, he tried his best to seem to know no more than she did when it came to Daniel, but he also wasn't about to sacrifice his son's comfort and happiness in the name of playing dumb.

One warm May afternoon, as he and Daniel were walking along, Lawrence couldn't help but think about the miraculousness of Daniel's new life in terms of the new life bursting forth all around them. He knew he was being corny and sentimental, but he also knew that being corny and sentimental was part of what being a new father was all about. Clichés that had once made him gag now seemed wise in their accuracy: his heart *did* flutter and hurt with love; he *did* see the world through brand new eyes; he *was* a changed man.

Though he understood that his son was too young for it to do him any good whatsoever, he identified everything for Daniel that crossed their path: mourning doves, fire hydrants, dandelions (he plucked one for Daniel to stroke with his tiny fingers; as soon as he tried to put it into his mouth, however, he had to take it away), bees, sparrows, starlings, maple trees, bicycles, sprinklers, alarm system signs, crickets, mayflies, doodlebugs, doggies hidden behind backyard fences (he couldn't help but visualize pit bulls lunging at the stroller, teeth bared, ears back), puffy clouds, and, at the corner of Crockett and Bowie, the neighborhood's only weeping willow, which hung over the sidewalk like a shredded curtain. As they pushed beneath it, Daniel giggled as the fronds trailed across his bare legs.

Rarely, Lawrence noticed, did he and Daniel ever see anyone out and about. He understood that this was probably because they always went for their walks at a time when most people were at work, but still. Not that he expected to see other men, though occasionally he ran across guys mowing lawns, trimming hedges, pruning trees. Usually, however, a battered pickup parked at the curb gave them away as hired help. Coming up on them sitting on a lowered tailgate during a water break, he'd sometimes catch them laughing, and he'd wonder what was funny. Was it a joke one of them had just told, or was it him? He'd give them a solemn nod in greeting, a nod that silently acknowledged the ridiculousness of a man pushing a stroller in the middle of a workday, and thus vindicate himself somewhat. Or at least that's what he hoped. Sometimes he felt the urge to say to them, "Hey, this isn't permanent, you know. I'll go back to work eventually, probably as soon as my son turns three. And I've got a degree, too. Do any of you losers have one?" Not that he'd ever do something like this, of course. For one thing, his degree in biology hadn't done him any good, so he hated ever even mentioning it—hated ever even *thinking* of it. But just imagining himself saying something like this always made him feel a little better.

Where, though, were the housewives, few though they may be? After all, not every household was a two-income household, as he well knew. The homemakers of this section of town just must not venture out much, he decided. The neighborhood was, after all, one of the oldest in Ivy. Most of the people seemed to be parents of college students who only came home for the holidays, their cars stuffed with dirty laundry, so it wasn't as if he expected to see many babies in strollers. Nevertheless, sometimes it was as if a neutron bomb had gone off, vaporizing the neighbors and leaving only vacant houses for him to stare at as he pushed his son through the stillness.

As he rolled up and down the aisles at Brookshire's on Monday mornings, doing the week's grocery shopping, Lawrence liked the looks and smiles he got from women when they spotted his baby son in the cart. He sensed their high regard (were *these* the invisible ladies from his neighborhood?) and imagined them thinking, "I wish *my* husband . . ."

He felt attractive in a way that he hadn't felt since . . . well, since never.

"How old is he?" they asked. "Oh, look at those lips! He's so beautiful."

Every woman said this about every baby, he understood, but he also knew that, indeed, his son was one handsome boy. All parents thought this about their children—they absolutely had to, right?—nevertheless, were Daniel anything less than perfect, he was pretty sure that he'd be mature enough to face facts if his son had jug ears or googly eyes or a freaky, pointed head. But, certainly, Daniel didn't. Fortunately, he looked just like his mother. He had her large, dark eyes (and they were darkening more by the day), her pinkish coloring, and even her dimples when he laughed. So when strangers failed to smile at Daniel, failed to acknowledge his stunningness, Lawrence found himself instantly hating them. Who could gaze upon Daniel and not be moved? Only the awful and stone-hearted.

And the women would talk to him through his son, as well: "Is your daddy taking care of you today? What a good daddy you have, taking you shopping! What a lucky boy you are to have such a sweet daddy!"

He saw the women eye the contents of his cart, too, saw the approval register in the slight nodding of their heads, the slight raising of their eyebrows at the sight of his entirely appropriate selections. For his son, Earth's Best Organic Whole Grain Rice Cereal, Naturally Preferred Organic Baby Food (garden peas, apple apricot, spinach carrot), Gerber Biter Biscuits, Pampers Swaddlers, Diaper Genie refills, and alcohol- and scent-free wipes. For him (and a wife? they asked themselves), salad fixings, bananas and oranges, broccoli florets and red bell peppers, a baguette from the bakery, salmon filets and butterfly pork chops. He imagined them marveling at what was not there, too: no beer, no frozen dinners, no pork rinds, no beef jerky.

And if his son fussed while they waited for their groceries to be rung up and sacked, he lifted him from his carrier and soothed him with pats on the back that could put any mother to shame. He was no Saturday-morning father, by God, one whose every interaction with his child was marred by clumsiness and indecision! No, he felt completely self-assured in his ability to ease and comfort his baby son.

Sometimes on their walks through the neighborhood, Lawrence imagined that the housewives he never saw nevertheless knew of him, watched for him, talked amongst themselves about him; he imagined himself famous amongst them, imagined himself known by them simply as *the father*, as in: "I saw the father with his son again today."

With phones pressed to their ears, they whispered to each other as they secretively peered through their blinds at him as he passed by:

"He's coming your way, Andrea. He just passed my house."

"He's early today. Yesterday, he didn't come by until after eleven."

Lawrence imagined them wondering what his story was. Was he married? If so, what the hell was up with his wife? Or was he—oh, no—was he gay, and the little one adopted? Or maybe he was independently wealthy—and divorced?

"I had my window open once, and I heard him whistling," one of them might say.

"What was he whistling?"

"'Twinkle, Twinkle, Little Star.'"

"Oh, how darling!"

Proud of the admiration he imagined himself receiving, Lawrence straightened his posture as he pushed his baby son north up Travis, west all the way down Crockett, south down Bowie, east all the way up Fannin, and back to Bonham.

Once, Lawrence dreamt that he was pushing Daniel's stroller along the quiet neighborhood's sidewalks. The weather starts out nice, but a heavy rain erupts. He and Daniel are on Bowie, as far from home as they can be. Lightning flares and thunder rumbles. Daniel yowls. Gripping the handle of the stroller tightly, Lawrence breaks into the fastest run he can manage without putting Daniel at risk. The rain beats down; puddles seem to emerge from beneath the surface of the sidewalk. His shirt clings to his skin, and his shoes fill with water while Daniel grows louder beneath the stroller's sodden hood.

A woman's voice calls from an open door—it's a dry square of light in the middle of the storm's wet darkness—*Come inside.* He does. The woman looks familiar though he doesn't know her. She's a redhead in stiletto heels wearing a full-length fur coat. Without a word, she wheels Daniel, who is now quiet, into another room. When she returns, she says to Lawrence, "I've been watching you, Daddy," and she lets the fur coat drop to the floor. Beneath it is another fur coat.

Usually he brought along the most recent issue of *The New Yorker* to read as they walked. It was a difficult thing to manage, though, reading and pushing Daniel. With his left hand, he guided the stroller down the sidewalk. With his right, he held the magazine folded in thirds so that the wind wouldn't whip the pages around. Each time that he reached the bottom of a column of text, he had to stop to refold the pages. Having to look up before crossing a street to another sidewalk further disrupted the continuity of both the walk and his reading, but if the weather was nice, Daniel was being good, and the article was interesting enough (which wasn't always the case, frankly), he didn't mind. Sure, sometimes he crashed into trash cans on pick-up days, startling Daniel, but it beat sitting in the house with no adult company other than the people who whispered to him from the television and the radio during naptime.

Though he hated to admit this to himself, he knew that he read *The New Yorker* more out of obligation than pleasure. Upon first meeting him, Bethany had been impressed that he had a subscription (a Christmas gift from his parents), so he'd never had the guts to abandon it. And then in the warehouse at Allied Medical Supplies, he'd come to be associated with it by his co-workers after he once made the mistake of bringing an issue into the break room.

"Hey, check it out," Ray, his supervisor, had said. "Too good for *Field & Stream* and *Hustler*, Mr. New Yorker? You do know we live in Texas, don't you?"

A number of others had been present to hear this. They laughed because, as Lawrence knew, everyone liked him less than they did Ray. And when Ray repeated the joke the next day as well, even though Lawrence hadn't brought *The New Yorker* back, the nickname stuck. It had been said as a joke—Lawrence knew this—but he also knew that it fit his reputation at work for being, as some of the guys sometimes said not so quietly behind his back, a bit "stuck on himself." Frankly, though, he didn't mind being identified with this phrase because, yes, he genuinely did think of himself as more intelligent than pretty much everyone who worked at AMS, at least in his department. They all seemed so dull, so content with the indistinguishable monotony of their weeks and months and years.

And so he had come to like thinking of himself as Mr. New Yorker. He swelled slightly when he heard one of his co-workers say, "Ask Mr. New Yorker, maybe he knows," though he'd deflate when he couldn't supply the information hoped for, as was the case most of the time, unfortunately.

Lying awake at night next to his sleeping wife, listening for the stirrings of his son in the next room, Lawrence found himself wondering when—or if—their life would ever return to how it had been prior to Daniel's arrival. He missed how he and Bethany had been able to do pretty much anything they wanted at any time they wanted. Like lying around on Sundays reading the newspaper. Like going to see movies. Like having sex. Mostly, though, he lay awake wondering what sort of father he would be. He wondered how he would manage to raise his son to be a boy, and then a man. He foresaw revisiting all the anxieties that had permeated his childhood as he watched them besiege his son. Or would they?

Besiege his son, that is. After all, Daniel was already huge—in the ninetieth percentile for height and weight, and had been so consistently since his first checkup. If only the good luck would continue. Maybe he'd escape his father's curse of always having to stand in the front row of every class picture, of always having the nurse make jokes about his hollow bones when she asked him to step onto the scale. Maybe he'd have no problems with bullies, no problems with sadistic coaches dead set on everyone showering after gym class, no problems with girls and the sickening anxiety they roused. But no matter how hard a son tried to be different from his father, didn't it seem that the most a son could ever really expect was merely to be a slight variation?

Sometimes Lawrence found himself whispering in the tiny shell of his son's ear, found himself saying, "I'm your father, Daniel. I'm your father. I'm your father." And it brought pleasure to him that doing such a simple thing brought so much pleasure to him, especially when Daniel smiled from the tickle of his father's breath against his skin.

But maybe, Lawrence sometimes wondered, maybe he loved his baby son too much. He considered this because occasionally he found himself having thoughts about Daniel that seemed, well, inappropriate. For example, he imagined himself taking bites out of him, devouring his flesh. He saw himself nibbling at his son's toes as if they were kernels from a corncob, chewing off his cheeks as if they were dumplings, gnawing away at his creased, fat thighs as if they were drumsticks. Was this normal? Did every parent experience such strange urges? Had his father? Maybe. But when he tried to picture his father looking down upon him with the same look that he felt on his own face when looking down upon Daniel, he couldn't see it. All he could see was how his father looked now: gray, creased, sour. Would his infatuation with Daniel fade, as his father's obviously had for him? Undoubtedly it was inevitable. But how horrible, he thought. And time was passing so fast, too. Already he found himself unable to recall exactly what Daniel had been like two months ago. Hell, a month ago! Already he was becoming too dependent on video and pictures to supplement his memory. While flipping through the pictures in the photo album, he found himself asking, *Was Daniel once really that small, that bald?* He found himself missing the son lying in his very arms, the Daniel that the following day would inevitably erase.

One May afternoon, Lawrence pushed his baby son's stroller along the quiet neighborhood's sidewalks because the weather had invited them to do so. It was a beautiful day, a wondrous day, a perfect day to make the Travis-Crockett-Bowie-Fannin-Bonham circuit. The sun was warm on top of his head, and because it was, he'd carefully massaged sunscreen into Daniel's sensitive skin. Folded in his back pocket was the latest issue of *The New Yorker*, the main article of which was an exhaustive examination of the uprising in Syria. He had skirted it for the last several walks, reading instead just about everything else, even the theatre review, but now there was nothing left to read, and he hated how woefully ignorant he was when it came to what was going on in that dusty part of the world, so when he peered beneath the stroller's hood and found a still and sleeping child, he pulled the magazine from his pocket, folded it into position, and began reading about a country that, despite all of the maps he'd seen on the evening news, he still couldn't picture very well. Soon enough, though, he was absorbed—and proud of himself, too, sure that he was the only person in Ivy, Texas, reading at that very moment all about Bashar al-Assad.

He didn't hear the bird singing from the branch that he and Daniel passed beneath, nor did he sense the sidewalk's slight decline as it sloped over the curb and into the alley that ran behind the houses on Bowie. When he caught a glimpse of the car—a flash of cherry and metal and glass—he instinctively jerked back on the stroller, so hard that it teetered to the left onto two wheels, nearly toppling over, and then the car was past.

The car had passed, and it had not hit the stroller.

The car had passed, and it had not hit Daniel, his baby son. Inches—by inches, it had missed. It had not hit his baby son.

His heart was a hot bubble in his chest.

The car continued down the street, its driver, having turned left from the alley onto Crockett, apparently oblivious to what had almost happened. Lawrence yelled incoherently, shaking the rolled-up *New Yorker* in the air, but he already understood that the anger he felt was directed just as much at himself as it was at the driver of the red Honda rolling merrily on its way.

Dropping *The New Yorker* to the ground, he checked on Daniel. His son slept on, unaware. And though he knew that Daniel would not have understood what had just happened even if he had been awake, Lawrence was thankful, nonetheless, that his son hadn't witnessed the incident. He then looked around at the windows of the nearby houses; they stared blankly back at him. No one else had seen it, either—thank God!—how he'd nearly pushed his son in front of a speeding car. Or maybe someone had, and now they were on the phone with Child Protective Services.

How could he have been so negligent? What if he had rolled into the alley a second sooner? Or if the Honda had been a second slower? Just as he'd once forced himself to eat a casserole that he'd carelessly let burn black in the oven, he forced himself to hear the thump and crunch of impact, to picture the mangled stroller and the dripping blood. He could continue his walk, he realized—after all, there was no way that anything like that could ever happen again because never again would he read while he pushed the stroller—but he deserved to be punished. He'd just lost his right to enjoy this fragrant May day any longer.

He crouched next to the stroller. Peering in at his sleeping son, he whispered, "Daddy's a bad daddy, Daniel. He's a bad, bad daddy."

And so, despite the beautiful weather and his sleeping son, he retrieved *The New Yorker* (he would have liked to have left it lying in the gutter for what it had nearly caused, but he knew that littering would nag at him later), turned around and headed toward home, a dull ache swelling from his testicles up to his stomach. For the very first time, he felt as if he'd failed in his duties as a father.

On their way home, Lawrence was still chastising himself for his unbelievable negligence when the sound of tires screeching on pavement caused him to look over his shoulder. A black sports car, straightening out of the fishtail it had skidded into as it made the turn onto Travis from Crockett, was hurtling in their direction. Lawrence watched it approach, listening to the rise in pitch of its engine. As he frequently did when he saw cars speeding through the neighborhood, he furiously recalled how he kept meaning to tell someone (the police? the city council?) that these streets were in desperate need of speed bumps. Without really realizing what he was doing, he stepped to the curb, plucked the rolled *New Yorker* from his back pocket, and started waving it like a wand as the car drew quickly closer.

"Slow down!" he yelled, and though he regretted it even as he was doing it, he hurled the magazine at the driver's darkly tinted passenger window, which it hit with an accuracy that shocked him.

Having just passed them, the car braked to an immediate halt, sending gray smoke up from its tires. The white reverse lights blinked on, and then the car slowly rolled backwards toward him. One of its tires stopped on *The New Yorker* now fluttering on the pavement. Lawrence stepped back onto the sidewalk, knowing that he never would have thrown the magazine had he not almost pushed Daniel in front of the Honda. Watching his contorted reflection sink into the car's door as the window lowered, he was surprised—and relieved—to see that the person behind the wheel was a woman, a cute blonde in a turquoise sweatshirt who looked to be no older than twenty-five.

"What's your fucking problem?" she shouted, leaning across her empty passenger seat. Coming out of such a pretty and delicate face, the language surprised him. "And what did you throw at me?

Jesus!"

"It was only a magazine," Lawrence said, embarrassed now, wishing that he'd just let the car drive on by. Feeling the vibration of the car's powerful engine rumbling up through the soles of his shoes, he wondered what kind of woman drove such a car. "The speed limit's thirty on this street."

"Who do you think you are? A cop or something?" She lifted a cigarette to her mouth and took a drag.

"Children live in this neighborhood." Lawrence pointed at Daniel's stroller. He hated how self-conscious she was making him feel, as if *he* had been the one behaving so irresponsibly. "You could have hit someone."

"Was I driving on the sidewalk?" She flicked the butt of her cigarette through the open window; it bounced smoking against the curb and fell back into the street.

"No, but—"

"Alright, then." She removed a fast-food drink from the cup holder on her dash and sipped from the straw. "It's my neighborhood, too, you know. I live on Bowie."

This news surprised him, that she wasn't just cutting through to Sam Houston, but he returned to the facts, feeling himself getting distracted and losing his sense of conviction. "But you had to be going at least forty-five, or fifty, and that's just . . . You might hit a kid one of these days if you keep driving like that."

"Any kid old enough to be playing in the street is in school right now."

"How do *you* know?" He felt his confidence coming back a bit with this. "Do you even know when the elementary schools let out for the day?"

"Do you?"

"No, I don't, but my son's only six months old. And I don't drive like you do."

"Well, I *do* know because my daughter's a second-grader. It's 3:15, and I'm on my way to pick her up."

As surprised as he'd been to hear that she was a neighbor, he was even more surprised to hear this, so surprised that his thoughts came out as words before he could stop them: "You're a *mother*?"

He saw the drink leave her hand, saw it coming toward him, but he couldn't imagine that she was actually throwing it, so he found himself unable to move quickly enough out of the way. When the cup hit him on the belt buckle, the lid popped off, and what remained of her cola splashed down the front of his pants. Ice cubes fell to the sidewalk, cracking.

All that he could manage to say was, "Hey! You . . ."

She disappeared behind the tinted glass, her face replaced by a reflection of his own shocked expression, and then drove off. By the time her car reached the end of the block, it was already going forty or more. After collecting *The New Yorker* and the woman's now-empty cup, he stepped over to her cigarette still smoldering in the street and ground it out violently with his shoe.

"You . . . bitch!" This word, hot in his mouth, was one that he never said, ever, but it felt good coming out—wonderful, actually—though he also felt guilty saying it, partly because he knew that, because of the Honda, he'd fully deserved to be hit with a half-full Coke.

After looking around to see if anyone had seen what had just happened (the street was no less dead than before), he checked to make sure that Daniel was still asleep, which, somehow, he was. And though he knew that Daniel would not have known what had just happened had he been awake, Lawrence was, nevertheless, yet again, thankful.

Once back inside the house, he threw away the woman's trash, along with *The New Yorker*—he definitely didn't give a damn about Syria now—and since Daniel was still asleep, he parked the stroller in the foyer so that he could go back to the bedroom to change his wet pants. He looked as if he'd wet himself. He had only one leg out of his khakis when the phone rang. Hopping as quickly as he could, he hoped to answer it before the noise woke Daniel, but before he was even within ten feet of the receiver,

Daniel began wailing, so he pulled up short and now in just his underwear, he hurried to the foyer so that he could unsnap his son from the stroller's harness and haul him up by the armpits.

"There, there," he said, patting Daniel on the back.

After his son's tears dwindled, Lawrence went to the answering machine, which was flashing with a message. It was Bethany checking in on them. Calling her back, he wondered if he'd feel compelled to tell her about what had happened, either the Honda or the other thing. He hoped not, though he hated how keeping secrets from her made him feel.

"I've only got a second," she said once the receptionist connected them. "I was just about to head to a meeting. How was your walk? Did you just get back?"

He hated when he caught her in a rush. He imagined co-workers crowding in the doorway of her office, pointing impatiently at their watches. "It was fine."

"How's he been?"

"Great."

"What an angel he is." She paused. "Well . . ."

"Yeah, you've got to go."

"I'll call you when I'm on my way home."

"Sure."

"You two have fun."

Lying awake next to his sleeping wife that night, Lawrence slowly slid from beneath the sheets and crept out of the bedroom with the clothes and shoes that he had secretively set out for himself before going to bed. After getting dressed in the black stillness of the living room, he slipped from the house and headed toward Bowie, by way of Travis and Crockett.

What he would do, he didn't quite know; all he knew was that he needed to do *something* once he got there and found the blonde's car.

The neighborhood's silence pressed against him as he walked as casually as he could manage down the sidewalks. The only sound was the rather distant thrum of a muscle car growling down the Sam Houston straightaway. And the only things to see were the occasional windows lit up blue by the flickering televisions of the neighborhood's insomniacs. How strange it was, he thought, walking these streets without Daniel in front of him. He missed the security that he found behind the mass of the stroller. But then he thought that, in a way, it was nearly as if Daniel were there, since what he was doing was almost as much for Daniel as it was for him.

When he turned onto Bowie, his pulse quickened. Hurrying down the sidewalk, scanning the cars lit just well enough by the streetlights to reveal their colors, he hoped he'd find hers parked on the street; if it was in the garage around the back, he'd be out of luck. Then, just as he was approaching the end of the block and fearing that he'd come for nothing, he spied the blonde's car parked in front of the second-to-the-last house on the left, a nondescript little home with dark brick and light trim that he and Daniel had undoubtedly passed dozens of times before. It sat there completely dark, oblivious to his presence. He pictured her sleeping peacefully in her bed, a breast unknowingly exposed to the air of the bedroom. Smiling, he approached her car, which he now saw was a sporty Mazda RX-8, and peered into its interior. There was nothing visible to give him any sense of who she was—no CDs, no mail, no trash (because she threw it all out, he thought bitterly, feeling again the wet shock against his thighs)—all there was to see was black leather and a black dashboard.

Quickly trying to determine his options, he looked from her car to her front door to the rest of the houses on Bowie. Though he rarely drank, he wished he were drunk, emboldened enough by alcohol to do something to be proud of in the morning. He imagined himself breaking in and sneaking down to her bedroom, but then he remembered that she had been on her way to pick up her kid, so that meant that she was probably married; the thought of a man lying next to her quickly killed his fantasy of standing at the foot of her bed, a shadowy menace.

After going back and forth between a few more reasonable possibilities, he eventually decided that he'd just kick in her taillights and headlights. Quick and simple. It wasn't as good as breaking her windshield or scratching the word *bitch* into the paint, but this was something he felt capable of doing, whereas, for whatever reason, the others seemed a bit beyond the scope of his daring. He scanned the nearby houses for possible witnesses. No lights were visible. No dogs were barking, no babies were crying for a feeding. He pictured Daniel lying in his crib and his wife lying in bed, and he hoped that his own house was as quiet as these here on Bowie. He would do it as quickly as he could, moving clockwise around the car, and as soon as all the lights were broken, he'd run like hell around the corner toward Fannin rather than return the way he had come. And then he'd be back in bed so quickly that it would be as if he'd never left it.

He positioned himself behind the brake lights on the right rear side, cocked his leg, and kicked as hard as he could. A piercing alarm erupted as soon as the plastic and glass shattered and fell to the pavement. Stunned that he had failed to consider this possibility, he took off, sprinting toward Fannin as fast as his body allowed, expecting to see every window that he passed explode with light.

Home, in the kitchen, he gulped down water straight from the tap and then wiped himself dry with paper towels. Once his heart finally returned to its normal rhythm, and once he was satisfied that police sirens and strobe lights were not going to erupt outside, he allowed himself to relax and think back on what he'd done. He was disappointed that he hadn't been able to kick out all of the car's lights, but he still felt pretty good. Smiling, he imagined the blonde coming out to her car in the morning to find the shards of her taillight lying on the pavement. Boy, was she going to be pissed. Or maybe she *wouldn't* see it; maybe she'd drive off and get pulled over on Sam Houston, and then she'd use that smart mouth of hers on the policeman, and he'd haul her to jail where she'd then get beaten up for looking at someone wrong.

"You shouldn't have messed with me, little lady," he whispered, pointing his finger at his pale reflection in the dark window over the sink.

Once his adrenaline faded, he realized he needed to get back to bed. It was late, and Daniel got up early. On his way down the hall, he stepped into his son's room, which glowed faintly orange from the duckling nightlight plugged in behind the rocker. He looked down at his son. Daniel was lying on his side, his arms wrapped around a blue elephant, his new favorite plushy. Watching his son's chest rise and fall until he was satisfied that all was fine, Lawrence had to fight the urge to reach down and stroke a lock of silky hair.

After whispering good night, he left the nursery feeling as if he had—at least a little bit—made up for the day's mistakes.

But back in bed, the good feeling began to fade. The kicking out of one taillight began to seem like less of a victory. It began to seem a little pathetic, particularly considering how much he'd been thinking about what had happened to him (getting splashed across the pants by a drink) and how little he'd been thinking about what he'd almost done to Daniel (pushing him in front of a speeding car). Covering his eyes with his arm to block out the streetlight's glare leaking through the gap in the curtains, he now wished he hadn't done anything at all.

Even if the weather more than allowed for it, he knew now that he wouldn't really feel like pushing Daniel's stroller along the quiet neighborhood's sidewalks in the morning. Would the neighborhood housewives miss him? Would they ask each other, "Have you seen the father with his son? I haven't. I hope they're okay." They would still go outside, he and Daniel would, because it was good for them to get sun and fresh air, and maybe in a week or so they'd venture out again, but for the time being, maybe they'd just stay within the safe confines of the backyard's fence, where the only threats would come from fire ants, the occasional mosquito, and the ultraviolet rays of the sun.

Bethany stirred, and then rolled toward him. "Have you been

up?"

"Yeah."

"Daniel?"

"No, he's fine."

She gently stroked his shoulder. "Trouble sleeping?"

He reached up and took her hand. "Yeah, I'm having some trouble."

The Woods of Tawakoni

Everett didn't think anything of it the first time it happened. He simply unlooped the sun-stiffened hose, squirted the mess from his top step, and then went back inside to have another cup of coffee.

For a week now he'd been unemployed, the victim of a downsizing that had cleaved more than it left, and for three months he'd been fifty-nine years old, which was a bad age to be without a job—too young to retire and too old to be attractive to just about everyone. Despite having quite a bit in savings, he blinked awake every night now, heart wobbling at the thought of being old and penniless within just a few years, living on nothing but tap water and cold soup. To calm his pulse, he reminded himself that he still had a few chits he could call in—in Houston, Austin . . . hell, even in Oklahoma City and Tulsa, if push came to shove. In the meantime, though, he needed to take advantage of this unanticipated downtime to rejuvenate. To relax. To enjoy himself, by God.

Enjoying himself meant escaping to the summer lake house on Tawakoni—the lake house that was neither on the lake nor a house; instead, it was just a trailer home fifteen minutes by foot from the waters of the Pawnee Inlet. And it wasn't summertime, either, as a matter of fact. The last of October's residual heat had faded, replaced by November's tangy chill. Gone were the jet skiers boiling the water and air with their thoughtless noise. On his walks, there was nothing to hear but the crunch and crackle of dead leaves beneath his shoes.

From the very beginning, the trailer had never been anything but strictly utilitarian. The furniture, what there was of it, had come from the piteous remains of garage sales on Sunday afternoons. The roof sagged, and the floor listed like a drunk beneath the indoor/outdoor carpeting. Soon enough the place would be practically uninhabitable, but it certainly had been wonderful once, despite the occasional cottonmouth encounter in the woods that pressed against its sides. And the ticks and chiggers, of course. Once upon a time, though, the three of them had come down at least twice a month during the summers to fish and water ski and nap in the hammock and build bonfires at night that sent smoke up to the stars that was like the very smell of peace, comfort, and happiness. . . .

But that was all a long time ago. His ex-wife, Lynn, now lived in Santiago, Chile, of all crazy places, married to a musician who apparently "wrung the last drops from every hour of every day," whatever that meant. And Josie, well, she'd gone her own way, as children were wont to do. She lived with her "partner" in an old house in Detroit, where she worked as a curator at an art museum. The last time they'd talked on the phone, she'd promised that it wasn't nearly as terrible up there as everyone said, but he couldn't help but picture her calling from a gray street strewn with abandoned cars, stove-in baby strollers, and bent hypodermic needles.

Enjoying himself also meant cutting himself off. He had brought along his cell phone, but he hoped not to have to turn it on. He was determined to "get back to nature." And, yes, he did hear quotation marks when he said these words in his head, because he understood how ridiculous it was to imagine himself roughing it while sleeping each night on a mattress and eating meals heated by a microwave, but still; this was as close as he could realistically manage. Twice already he'd taken the boat out in search of catfish hiding in the shadows of the willows, though certainly not as systematically or efficiently as his summertime neighbors. Nevertheless, he still managed to reel in a few big enough to bring back to filet, fry in cornmeal, and eat with hush puppies and black-eyed peas, which heartened him a little, at least for an hour or two.

Enjoying himself also meant not letting himself think about anything while doing nothing more than reading outside in a lawn chair. As a treat to himself, before leaving Dallas, he'd stopped at a used bookstore and snatched up every Hemingway on the shelf. The idea had come to him while skipping through cable channels at three in the morning the night before. Happening upon Bogie and Bacall in *The Big Sleep*, he'd thought of their first film together, *To Have and Have Not*, and that was all it had taken.

Back when he was eighteen, just like every other student at Texas Tech, he'd been required to take a survey course in American literature. According to the catalogue, the class was supposed to cover authors from the Civil War to the present, but his professor, Dr. Patton, announced on the first day of class that he had no desire to discuss the likes of Stephen Crane, Mark Twain, or Henry James. "Nor," he added, "T. S. Eliot or William Carlos Williams, much less Emily Dickinson or Edna St. Vincent Millay. All I intend to discuss is Ernest Hemingway. Because, as far as I'm concerned, Hemingway *is* American literature. So if you don't like the sound of that, drop the course." A number of students maneuvered their way down the crowded aisles toward the exit, but Everett stayed, more out of laziness than anything. Then, unexpectedly, as the weeks passed, he became enraptured. Oh, the man's life! And his sentences! "Lapidary," Dr. Patton called them, and Everett had to pull out his dictionary to discover how perfect this word was.

But sadly, he eventually had to ask himself the inevitable question: to what end? To what purpose? As much as he had fallen in love with Nick Adams, Jake Barnes, and Frederic Henry, he begrudgingly abandoned them for more bankable realities (his major was business administration, after all), but not before swearing to himself that one day, once he had made his fortune and sat comfortably on a golden executive throne, he'd return to Paris, to Les Deux Magots. . . .

The second time, he nearly stepped in it. After sliding his bifocals onto his forehead, he squatted in order to see it better. It looked a bit like the remains of an overturned bowl of oatmeal, though paler, and with flecks of red here and there. And just as he'd done the first time, he squirted it into the dead grass with the hose and then went back inside to have another cup of coffee.

Ever since coming out to the lake house, he had slept like a baby. Like a log. Like the dead. It was as if he would fall down an abandoned well. Stiff and numb, he'd wake ten hours later with his book open and the lamp still on. He knew, of course, that dreams must still be visiting him every night, but the well was dark and deep, so he never remembered any of them.

One morning, however, he woke up troubled by a dream that he couldn't reel up before it disappeared into the depths. A fuzzy unpleasantness fluttered between his organs. After splashing icy water on himself, he stared at the wet face in the bathroom mirror, wondering what it had been about, and it was then that he remembered a postcard that his daughter had sent him once from a museum somewhere in Europe, a postcard of a painting, and the painting had been of a man looking into a mirror. But instead of looking at a reflection of his face, the man could see only a reflection of the back of his own head, as if he were somehow standing both behind and in front of himself. The way that the artist had so easily made strange something as normal as a man looking into a mirror had disturbed him in an inexpressible way, leaving him feeling strangely weak. He'd wondered at the time whether Josie had meant something by sending it to him, or had it simply been a random choice in the gift shop? On the back, she'd written only, *Having a great time – Love, Josie.*

The third time: he stepped out to breathe in his favorite moment of the day—the cool, thick dampness of morning that sagged between the oaks like a heavy web—and his bare right foot sank into it. It squeezed up cold and thick between his toes. He yelped in surprise at the sensation, then hopped one-legged down to the dirt so that he could wipe his sole clean. Cursing loudly in the silence, he looked back at the mashed lump on his top step. It looked the same as the first two times—like oatmeal. Or the partially digested head of a stringy mop. And the red flecks? Definitely blood, he could tell that now.

The first two times had been worthy of a frown and a furrowed brow as he dispersed the mass with bursts of thumb-pressured water from the garden hose, but nothing more. A third time, though? That was downright bizarre. What the hell was slinking out of the woods of Tawakoni to vomit on his doorstep like this?

Since the bookstore hadn't had *In Our Time* (or *any* anthology of Hemingway's stories, for that matter), he started with *The Sun Also Rises*, as Dr. Patton would have demanded. Before opening to the first page, however, he wondered whether he would love it just as much as he had as an undergraduate, or would he find that, as with so many things, it was better not to revisit the passions of youth? Time and age, he found, had an unpleasant way of spoiling what should be left alone to shine on unchanged in memory. Take Lynn, for instance. Had their marriage not ended so viciously—had they never even married at all, maybe—he might still be able to take pleasure in his recollection of her during those early months of their fanatic lust and love, but all of that had been irrevocably poisoned by the acrimony of the more recent past. Would Hemingway suffer similarly? In light of all that had happened since those days when his body had bulged with muscles and his once-golden hair had hung to his shoulders, Everett wondered if his strong feelings for Papa would now seem foolish and embarrassing. He nearly didn't want to find out.

A *fourth* time. He could ignore this no longer.

Waiting for catfish in the quiet stillness of Mulberry Cove, Everett found himself thinking of a Nick Adams story. In it, Nick camps on the banks of a river after coming back from the war. For pages and pages, Everett remembered, the story is nothing but long descriptions of Nick building campfires, Nick boiling coffee, Nick cooking flapjacks, Nick baiting hooks with grasshoppers, Nick fishing for trout. Dr. Patton had explained that Hemingway wrote it like this to emphasize how Nick was avoiding his painful memories of the war by occupying himself with activities and sensations that he associated with a more innocent and happy time in his life. Initially, Everett had found the story tedious, but this explanation made such immediate sense to him that, despite the heat of the room, goosebumps had sprouted across the skin of his arms. And now here he was, in amongst the cattails with his spinning rod, his number six treble hooks, his slip corks, his punch bait, and his cooler full of ice in anticipation of his catch, breathing in the pleasantly muddy smell rising up around him and suddenly remembering tiny Josie sitting with him on the banks of the Sabine River, bamboo fishing poles in their hands.

What other choice did he have? After dark, he would set himself up in the lawn chair on the porch, and beneath the yellow bulb, he'd read as late as he could manage. Either he'd catch sight of whatever it was that was slipping out of the woods at night, or he'd scare it off simply by sitting there. And just in case, beneath his chair he'd set his shotgun, which he hadn't fired in years.

Ketchum, Idaho. After so long, why did he still remember the place where Hemingway had killed himself? He could barely remember what his own daughter looked like, and yet he could remember the name of the town in which a man he never knew had ended his life with a twelve-gauge blast to the head. What had Dr. Patton said about it? That there had been no other choice.

"Don't you see?" he'd said. "Papa couldn't die a frail old man, and that was exactly what he was becoming. He *had* to die on his own terms. It was *not* a cowardly act, no matter what anyone has ever said or written or thought. It was *not.* It was admirable. It was beautiful. It was *good.*"

The first night, Everett, in a wool sweater holed by moths, settled in with a full thermos of piping hot coffee and the final book from his stack, *Death in the Afternoon*, which he'd never read despite Dr. Patton having assigned it. It had seemed so boring at the time. Three hundred pages about nothing but bullfighting? Plus a hundred pages of glossary for all the Spanish terms used? No thanks, he'd said, not when Nora Most in Biology finally seemed to be paying at least as much attention to him as she was to the fetal pig they were dissecting together. But now, he was really enjoying the stories about Juan Belmonte and Joselito, the bravest and most graceful of the matadors, who flirted with death in order to deliver, with utmost dignity, the final *estocade* high up between the animal's shoulder blades while leaning over the imminent approach of its fatal horns. And instead of useless, the vast number of terms now seemed beautiful in their particularity. *Coleta*: the braided pigtail that all matadors wore at the back of the head. *Banderillas* and *picas*: the harpoon-like spears (one long, one short) thrust into the bull's withers to weaken the muscles of its neck. *Cornada*: a wound caused by the penetration of the bull's horns. And then the photographs! Though blurry and gray, the matadors still seemed so noble all these many decades later, so stoic in their willingness to confront the enraged bulls so nakedly. He found himself flipping to their pictures again and again, to stare at how close to death they readily stood, with nothing in their hands but a fluttering cape.

Nothing happened the first night. At four in the morning, he had gone inside and slept until noon. Tonight, he finished *Death in the Afternoon* a few minutes before midnight. After looking one last time at the photos of Chicuelo, Luis Freg, and El Gallo (all long gone now, but still frozen here in vibrant life, mere centimeters from death's gory points), he set the book under his lawn chair next to his flashlight and shotgun.

Since the bulb above him is only sixty watts, all he can see of the woods that start fewer than fifteen feet away is a vaguely thicker darkness upon an already thick darkness. In a globe of fragile yellow light, staring blindly into nothingness with a cooling thermos of coffee in his hand, he wonders what's out there. Part of him wants nothing to happen so that he can return to his usual routine, but another part of him wants whatever it is that's been doing this to finally just crawl out and reveal its damn self. Probably it's nothing more than a sickly possum or raccoon. But what if it's a rabid coyote? Does he have the nerve to shoot to kill?

He turns the porch light off, leaving himself sitting in what now seems, illogically, a slightly chillier darkness. The silence is loud in his ears. Though the flashlight now lies in his lap, he won't turn it on unless he hears something approaching. He stares into the black, blinking . . . listening . . . and thinking, mainly about reading Hemingway. As a student, how had he not picked up on the man's obsession with death? He could recall being affected by Catherine Barkley and her baby dying at the end of *A Farewell to Arms*, but what about everything else? Robert Jordan dying at the end of *For Whom the Bell Tolls*. The suicide in the Nick Adams Indian story that he somehow remembered. Even that fishing story had death in it; it's what haunts Nick as he fishes and fishes and fishes, hoping to keep his mind clean and clear.

The darkness before Everett's eyes disappears as other stories from his sunny days in college come back to him. The one set on a safari hunt that ends with a man getting shot by his wife, maybe not accidentally. The one about the two men who come to town to kill a man . . . the Swede! They eat at a café while they wait for him. And then that one with the man patiently dying from gangrene in Africa. He and a woman are waiting for a plane to rescue him. While vultures circle above, the man senses death creeping toward his cot to sit on his chest and blow its rotten hyena breath into his face.

A noise. Something somewhere in the stillness makes a noise. Everett stares walleyed, hoping to hear it again. Hoping not to, also. Without blinking, he waits, breathing quietly, listening. There it is again—a rustling, a crackling, on a night with no wind. He wants to turn on his flashlight, but no, he can't; he has to be strong, wait for whatever it is to move closer. He can't scare it off just yet.

He turns it on. A cone of icy light reveals nothing but tree trunks and their lurching shadows. Slowly he pulls the light to the left, to the right, to the left again. There's nothing to see but darkness, which somehow seems even darker now that it's illuminated.

Standing with the flashlight in one hand and his shotgun in the other, he moves slowly and carefully down the steps and toward the trees, trying not to jiggle the flashlight, which makes the shadows leap unpleasantly, like living things that normally stay hidden behind the oaks. As a little girl, Josie used to beg him to let her explore "the fairy forest," as she called it, but he never let her, imagining her losing her way, getting bitten by a snake, or breaking her leg in a fall and being too far away for him to hear her cries.

God, he hasn't seen her in so long now. Once, years ago, the last time she flew back to Texas to see him, they went to the Kimbell Museum in Ft. Worth, and he remembers how he watched her as she stared with so much focus at the paintings, and how he felt such a startling sense of wonderment that this woman before him—so cultured and sophisticated and intelligent—could have come, if only in part, from him.

He wonders if she's called his cell recently. Maybe, but probably not. He knows that she loves him—and he hopes that she understands how much he loves her—but how long has it been since they've actually talked, and not merely mouthed safe, easy, empty words to each other? He knows that he's entirely to blame, and he hates himself for his inflexible ways and opinions, but what to do? The long years lived apart—physically, emotionally—have thickened and hardened so much that he can't imagine ever breaking through. Nevertheless, in the morning he determines to turn on his cell phone and call her. In the meantime, he imagines the message that he'd love to find waiting for him: "You sure are a hard man to get hold of, you know that, Daddy? I haven't talked to you in a month of Sundays. What's keeping you so busy? I hope something fun. Regardless, call me! And if you don't, I might have to call the police to make sure you're okay, and I know you don't want that!"

He's been walking for five minutes now, pausing every few seconds to listen. For a moment he turns off the flashlight to feel the darkness push against his face, but then he thinks of the batteries dying, or something taking advantage of the light's absence to rush toward him, and he quickly turns it back on. Relieved to see that everything looks as it did moments earlier, he adjusts his grip on the shotgun, wondering now how he expects to shoot anything while holding the flashlight, and then decides it's time to head back to the lake house because there's obviously nothing out here in the woods but him. Whatever he heard wasn't anything more than the natural sound of a tree sagging to rest for the night. Following the bobbing ghost of light radiating from his hand, he turns around.

He doesn't like the thought of turning his back on whatever it is that he's still fairly sure isn't really out here with him, but he refuses to look over his shoulder. He just starts walking faster, imagining Hemingway striding back to camp for another shot of whiskey, disappointed that the sound he'd heard in the savannah's darkness hadn't been a beast begging to have its head mounted on a wall in Key West.

When he calls Josie tomorrow, he'll ask her about that story with the man dying of gangrene, because he knows that she'll know, being the brilliant woman that she is, even though he also knows that, before giving him the answer, she'll sigh and then call Hemingway a "misogynistic prick" or something similar.

What's it called, Josie? And what got there first: the plane or the hyena?

He hears something behind him—a cracking snap, the sound of something heavy breaking something fragile—and knows that he's fallen into its trap. Without whirling around in an attempt to pin the intruder with his glowing beam, without attempting for even a lone second to stand tall in the face of a mysterious danger as Hemingway would have, he runs, ignoring the low flames of the chili he ate for dinner licking upwards from his stomach. Oh, Jesus, can he outrun it? He pushes his legs to pump faster, regretting having ever, ever left his porch. The shotgun, heavy in his right hand, he lets fall, knowing that he can come back for it when the sun comes up. Squinting into the darkness cut by the zigzag trails of his flashlight's bucking ray, he curses himself for not having turned the porch light back on before leaving. Lord, how appreciated a yellow beacon would be right now!

This is what he's thinking at the moment that his left foot clips a root, and his body leaves the ground, arcing silently through the air. . . .

He doesn't feel himself land, nor does he feel his skull crack against a sharp rock jutting from the dirt. Sinking slowly through his own black, personal waters, he's still running, but he's no longer lost, and the beast is no longer snapping at his heels. Past the desiccated hammock hanging now from only one tree, past the shed full of abandoned summer gear—water skis, life vests, badminton racquets and shuttlecocks—past the crippled picnic table where he and Lynn and Josie used to eat watermelon on hot afternoons, he races toward the clean steps leading to his trailer door, behind which he can hear his cell phone ringing. It's a call coming from Detroit, twelve hundred miles away, and he knows that it won't stop ringing, no matter how long it takes for him to reach it.

Congee

I walked into Osage Medical because it was the only place in my health plan's directory still accepting new patients, at least in the Sharpstown part of Houston. When the receptionist said I'd be seeing Dr. Lee Wynn, I of course had no reason to think that I wouldn't be seeing someone similar to myself—after all, could there *be* a more normal-sounding name? So when the door of the examination room finally slid open fifteen minutes later, I admit I was bit shocked to see a Vietnamese woman step inside.

"Good afternoon, Mr. Funk," she said. "I'm Dr. Wynn."

"Good afternoon," I echoed as casually as I could manage while trying to tie the name that I'd been given with the person before me. But then I saw the identification badge clipped to the pocket of her white coat—above its tiny picture of her face was written *Dr. Ly Nguyen.*

Marveling at my stupid assumption, I thought back through all the doctors I'd seen over the years, all the general practitioners and the specialists, the dentists and the optometrists. With all the different types of people in the medical profession these days, how had I managed never to be seen by anyone but white males? More importantly: how the hell was I going to get through this—having a woman examine me—without dying of humiliation or making a fool of myself?

"Born in 1961?" she asked me, reading through the forms that I'd been asked to fill out as a new patient. She had only the slightest hint of an accent. "So . . . forty-nine years old?"

"Yes." I tried not to move on the examination table's noisy butcher paper despite the fever chills making me shiver.

"Single, yes?"

"Yes," I said, wondering how she might interpret this bit of information. Would she figure I was divorced? An unlovable scumbag? A homosexual? A virgin scared to death of women?

Without looking away from my file, she sat down on a wheeled stool, resting the soles of her tennis shoes on its bottom rung. "Mother still alive and in good health?"

"Yes," I said, not wanting to get into all that had gone to hell with Momma because of her diabetes. I'd come to Osage Medical because I felt like shit, not to map the genetics of my family tree.

"Father deceased?"

"Yes," I said, grateful that I'd only put *accident* as the cause of death instead of the truth, which was that he'd been killed at the Battle of Ong Thanh.

"Was the accident a recent one?"

"No, I was only six."

Without a word of condolence, she flipped through more pages, pausing occasionally. "No recreational drugs? No alcohol consumption? No smoking?"

"No," I said, lying three times with only one word, though not terribly, at least not to the first part.

"No family history of heart trouble, stroke, cancer, or psychiatric illness?" She said this as if she didn't quite believe what I'd marked down.

"Nope." I'd checked the *No* boxes all the way down that page without bothering to read a word.

"Do you exercise regularly?"

I wanted to lie again, but how could I? Wasn't it obvious that I didn't? "No."

"You should, you know." She looked up at me for the first time since absorbing herself in my medical history. "You're not overweight, but . . . " She moved her hands in small circles above the buttons of her white coat, subtly suggesting the slight flabbiness of my belly, and then she wrote a few final notes in my file before closing it. "Regardless, you seem pretty healthy. On paper, at least." She stood and approached me. "So, why are you here, Mr. Funk?"

I told her about the sore throat and fever that had already caused me to miss two days of teaching at my new school, Strake Jesuit.

Armed with a tongue depressor and one of those tiny lights that she would later use to look into my ears and nostrils, she peered into my open mouth. "Mmmm."

"That good, huh?" I said once she'd lifted the bitter-tasting wood from my tongue. I knew that I wasn't being funny, but her wordlessness made me nervous.

"Looks like strep throat, but we'll know in a couple of minutes." She came at me now with a cotton swab on the end of a stick, which she poked against both of my tonsils and the back of my throat, nearly making me gag. After taking it to the counter behind her and doing something with it, she returned to listen to my heart and lungs. I breathed deep and slow as she moved the cold disc of her stethoscope over my chest and back . . . how horrible it was to have a woman touch my hairy, out-of-shape body.

"I bet I've also got walking pneumonia," I said, wanting to disrupt the awkwardness of being so close to her that I could feel her body's heat. "And probably the boogie-woogie flu, too, right?"

"Lie back now, Mr. Funk," she said, ignoring me, her firm hands easing me down onto the table as if she were going to give me a massage.

"Okay," I said, unable to say no. The paper crackled beneath me.

"How long ago was your last exam?"

"I don't remember, honestly," I said, feeling appropriately guilty as I stared up at the fluorescent lights, avoiding her eyes.

Just below my belt that she'd asked me to loosen, she palpated my spongy abdomen, feeling the contours of my various internal organs. Meanwhile, breathing in her antibacterial perfume, I slowly lowered my gaze from the ceiling until I was staring at her pretty neck, watching a vein (or maybe an artery) pulsing unhurriedly.

I've never thought the Vietnamese to be an attractive people. This was what I was idly mulling over on my drive to the pharmacy to turn in my antibiotics prescription. (She'd been dead-on about the strep throat.) What was it exactly that made most of them so ugly? After all, how different were they from the Japanese, who had some of the most beautiful women on the planet? Regardless, there had been something about Dr. Nguyen that appealed to me, though I couldn't exactly say what it was. Most of the time when I find a woman lingering in my thoughts, there's usually a fairly precise reason—her face, her breasts, her ass—but nothing had particularly stood out with her except maybe the dainty shells of her unpierced ears and a scar the size and shape of a 1/0 jig hook on one cheek. Nonetheless, I couldn't quite shake her. Maybe it was the fever making me loopy. Or maybe it was simply because she seemed like someone I might have a chance with. Not that I was a hopeless case or anything. I'd had plenty of girlfriends over the years, some pretty serious, though none in awhile. Hell, I'd even been engaged to be married at one point.

By nature, I've always been shy and a bit socially awkward, so the usual steps of the dating ritual—the flirting, the asking for the phone number, the calling for the date—have never come easily for me, but even when I've managed to succeed, the good times have generally been pretty short-lived. It's been my fault, typically, but sometimes it's been theirs. Other times, though, it's been my mother's.

Believe it or not, most women tend not to find a man all that attractive when his mother lives with him—or, to be more accurate, when he lives with his mother, since our house is the same one that she and my father bought in 1957 and that I grew up in. Not that it really matters. No matter how you spin it, I still give off the smell of one of those lonely, middle-aged men shacked up with his elderly mother. I don't fit the general stereotype, though. I'm not angry at the world. I'm not stockpiling weapons in preparation for a workplace rampage. I'm not a conspiracy nut; I don't think the Jews were behind the 9/11 attacks so as to spur the U.S. into a war against the Arab world. I don't play *Second Life* or *World of Warcraft* (though I'll admit to trying out both). Hell, I don't even play fantasy football. I'm just a high school history teacher whose mother's been on full disability for fifteen years because of her diabetic retinopathy (she's blind, in other words) and, more recently, her footless left leg, thanks to a necessary amputation.

Speaking of my mother, I didn't dare tell her that the doctor I ended up seeing was Vietnamese because she continues to blame them for pretty much everything that's gone wrong with her life over the last forty-plus years. She's justified in blaming them for the death of her husband, of course (at least the Viet Cong, that is), but she blames them for lots of other things, too—her inability to remarry, her diabetes, the decline of Sharpstown, and God knows what else—as if all of these things became inevitable the moment a VC's bullet pierced my father's skull nine thousand miles away on the very same day that—I kid you not—*Hair* premiered on Broadway. *Oh, those goddamned gooks*, she mutters, staring into her private darkness. *Those goddamned boat people. Of all the places in the world, why did they all have to come here? It's because of how hot it is. So hot and steamy—like a jungle. Makes them feel at home, I'm sure. And then the fish, of course. I know how much those people love their fish, but they have no right coming here and taking over Galveston Bay like they've done. No right . . .*

When I got home, I found her sitting next to her radio, listening to KTRH, News Radio 740, as always. Recognizing the pompous voice of Rush Limbaugh grumbling from the speakers, I asked, "What's the burr under his saddle today?"

"Did you know there are eleven *million* illegal aliens in this country?"

"Is that all?"

"What do you mean, *Is that all?* Those eleven million aliens cost this country over a hundred billion a year to take care of. That's 'billion' with a 'B.'"

I waved the bag of Sonic cheeseburgers under her nose. "Are you ready to eat?"

She grabbed the bag and promptly unwrapped a cheeseburger while continuing on about how we needed to amend the Fourteenth Amendment pronto in order to stop illegal aliens from coming over here and having anchor babies.

"What the hell are anchor babies?" I asked, picturing tiny, diapered things run through with giant hooks and then tossed overboard into the Gulf.

"They're the brats those aliens come over here to have so that they'll be born American citizens. Then the mothers, you see, they go and apply for visas in order to stay here and take care of them." She sneered. "You think you're so much smarter than me, but see? You didn't even know what those crafty bastards are up to, did you?"

With my cheeseburger and fries, I walked quietly out of the room and down the hall.

"Did you?" she called out louder, somehow knowing that I had left. "Did you?"

My father enlisted in 1966. I don't know why, exactly. Momma said that it was because he was patriotic and hated the Communists, but I don't know if I believe that anymore. The older I get, the more I think it might've been simply to get away from her. And maybe me, too. Who knows? I don't remember him too well, to be honest, though I suppose that's not surprising. After all, I was only five the last time I saw him. Besides the photographs that I still have of him—most with him squinting unsmilingly into sunlight—very little has stayed with me. But I do remember us playing card games—Slapjack, Spit in the Ocean, War. Or at least I think I do. I remember how his rough fingers smelled of tobacco and motor oil. I remember him at Steward

Beach, trying to teach me to swim in the surf . . . and how I sensed his disappointment at my fear of both the relentless waves and all the unknowable things swimming beneath and around me. I remember the sleeves of his shirts rolled up tight at his biceps, accentuating their sinewy strength. And that's about all he left me with, really, besides the things Momma didn't sell, throw away, or lose—his burial flag, his tackle box full of lures and spinners and treble hooks, his father's arrowhead collection laid out on green felt, the horseshoe cufflinks that he wore on the day he married Momma.

From what I've managed to piece together, he seems to have been a thoroughly ordinary man, the sort who probably didn't make much of an impression on most people. He stayed on the path—a God-fearing Southern Baptist who voted Republican every four years and who liked to drink Pearl Beer on the weekends and go watch the Buffs play whenever the weather was nice, especially if it was a doubleheader. He worked as a mechanic at R.C.'s Garage on Harwin. Momma pointed it out to me once, or at least where it once had been. It's a bar now called The Happy Cortez, or something just as stupid. The sign outside advertises pitchers of Miller Lite for only five bucks during Happy Hour.

I hate the word *vibe*—it makes me think of stupid hippies, peace signs, and flower power—but *vibe* was the word that initially came to mind when I thought of Dr. Nguyen. More accurate words came to me later, however, words like *ease* and *comfort.* Hardly as sexy as *vibe*, granted, but when you're forty-nine, what *is* sexy anymore? Ease and comfort might not be as exciting as the young flesh that runs past me at Lansdale Park while I sit under a tree grading sophomore tests on the Revolutionary War, but there's something to be said for the simplicity and straightforwardness that maturity brings in larger measures each passing year. She obviously knew that I was single, and I knew that she was, too, since the ring finger on her left hand was bare. Had she been in her twenties, none of this would have meant anything whatsoever, but Dr. Nguyen was no spring chicken, as my mother might have said once, before she permanently lost her good spirits. There was no ignoring the crow's tracks that had made their short but significant way from the corners of her eyes to her temples, the faint lines that creased the flesh below her cheeks. As she examined me that first time—her hands, my body—I felt a pleasant sagging in the area of my heart, a relaxation.

So, I'll admit it: after that, I cooked up reasons to schedule appointments.

The first of these subsequent visits, however, was entirely legitimate; I went in to see about a mole on my shoulder that had grown a bit in size over the years. Its edges were slightly uneven, as well, which I knew could sometimes mean something bad. She leaned toward me to examine it through a pair of funky glasses that she slid from the breast pocket of her white coat, so close that I could feel twin streams of cool air against my skin as she breathed out through her nose, and then she told me that I had nothing to worry about but that we should keep an eye on it, nevertheless.

While waiting to see her about this mole, I did wonder if I had only imagined the gently charged air during my strep visit, but she immediately put me at ease by touching me on the arm, smiling, and saying, "How are you feeling, Mr. Funk? All better?" Although from there we didn't say much to each other beyond the parameters of my visit's ostensible purpose, she did seem impressed when she saw that I'd lost a few pounds, and not simply in the way that a doctor might be impressed by the efforts of a patient—no, also in the way that any woman is impressed by a man taking charge of a situation, taking responsibility. I'd stopped eating the food from Sonic that Momma made me buy her for dinner—the chili cheese dogs, onion rings, chicken nuggets, and cheeseburgers—and started eating things like veggie burgers and salads with balsamic vinegar dressing. I'd even started jogging in the neighborhood a few evenings a week, and as I passed the fancy, new condominiums a few blocks from the house, I imagined Dr. Nguyen looking down from one of the windows and seeing me glowing in the haloes of the streetlights, valiantly chasing my old life away.

My next visit concerned a wart on the pinkie of my left hand. I'd had it for years and never given two thoughts about it. She froze it off just like that.

The following visit was even less defensible: I went in with the complaint of a muscle twitching in my left cheek. Which was a lie. Well, not a total lie; I'd had muscle twitches there before, but none recently. Besides, I knew from reading about them on Web MD that they were no big deal and that there was nothing a doctor could really do about them, but that didn't stop me from making an appointment for the very end of the day on a Friday.

"Is it twitching now?" she asked, approaching me.

"You know," I said, "it did all day today while I was teaching, but it stopped about twenty minutes ago, if you can believe it. Just to spite me, of course. I'm sure it'll start up again just as soon as I get back in my car, too."

She touched my cheek with two fingers and massaged it tenderly. "Muscle fasciculation is very common."

"It sounds terrible when you call it that." I imagined a muscle twitching beneath the mysterious hook-shaped scar on her own cheek and wondered how she had gotten it. Had it been some sort of accident on the boat over, when she was a little girl? "I think I like *twitch* better."

She smiled and nodded as she returned to her stool.

"I've never had one last this long before or drive me this crazy," I said, determined not to let an uncomfortable silence settle between us. "When it gets going, I swear, it feels like a bullfrog in there."

She told me how these twitches typically were caused by a lack of sleep, not drinking enough water, or stress. I told her that I got plenty of sleep and drank plenty of water, so when she asked if I was under stress, I laughed inside, thinking of the bitter pain in the ass waiting at home to tell me more about what a shithole the city of Houston, the state of Texas, and the nation of America had become, thanks to all the people here who didn't belong. Should I play it cool and just say, *No, not particularly*? Or should I use the opportunity to open up, to tell her something true about myself? After all, didn't the Vietnamese revere their elders—and dedicate themselves to their care—just as the Chinese and the Japanese were so famous for doing?

"Stress with work?" she suggested. "Or with family, maybe?"

"Well," I said, still unsure whether I would say it. "There is my elderly mother. She lives with me so that I can take care of her. Sometimes that's a bit stressful. She's not exactly an easy person to deal with."

When she didn't say anything, I immediately regretted saying this, imagining her mentally striking my name through with a red pen. But then she rolled closer on her wheeled stool, and I sensed suddenly that my appointment had just ended—officially, at least. The week was closing down along with the day, and now it felt as if she might just want to talk, to relax a bit before leaving Osage Medical to return to her clean, quiet home until Monday morning.

"Have you thought about putting her in an assisted-living facility?" Her voice was now quieter than before, less authoritative.

Had I thought about it? Hell, I'd *fantasized* about it endlessly but never seriously considered it. As long as Momma could make do while I was at school during the day, I couldn't allow myself to do such a thing. No matter how heavy a chain she was around my neck, she was still my mother, the woman who had raised me by herself ever since that day Daddy kissed me on the head and then waved goodbye for the very last time. "No, not really."

She pushed herself closer, and the stool's wheels squeaked beneath her. "I admire you for that. So many people are happy enough to pass responsibility on to someone else, especially someone they can pay."

Hearing this, I felt my cheeks warm, but I didn't know how to respond. Should I say *Thank you*? Should I say how much I loved my mother? I settled for a shrug of the shoulders, hoping to look modest but in agreement.

"My sister has been taking care of our father like you're taking care of your mother," she said, staring intently into my eyes, "but she's about to put him in a nursing home because she says it's all gotten too difficult to handle. And what's sad is that I'm too far away to do anything about it."

Someone tapped tentatively on the door and said Dr. Nguyen's name.

Watching her face turn away from me as I pictured her father, a frail Ho Chi Minh lying in bed next to a window looking out onto a stand of green bamboo, I sensed her intense annoyance at the interruption.

"What is it?" she asked.

"Dr. Dudek is in need of your assistance, if you have a moment."

Before rising from her stool, Dr. Nguyen put her hand on my knee for a heartbeat longer than was appropriate for a professionally friendly gesture of farewell.

"Take care of yourself, Mr. Funk," she said.

Contemplating the potential meaning of this extra second of pressure as I walked out to my car, I immediately began planning my next ailment.

In all my life, I had never tasted Vietnamese food, but on my way to Sonic for Momma's dinner after leaving Osage Medical, I stopped at a place called Que Huong. Being neither an impetuous person nor an adventurous eater, I was proud of my spontaneous decision to try something so alien. I hadn't yet thought about whether or not I would later tell Dr. Nguyen about my visit to the apparently popular place next to Lotus Pharmacy, but feeling my attraction to her intensifying, I wanted to know more, even if it involved nothing beyond eating the strange food of her culture.

Inside, a silent but smiling young man in black pants and a white shirt led me to a small table with only one chair. He filled my water glass and handed me a menu while I looked around at the framed photographs on the walls of what I assumed to be Vietnamese landscapes—waterfalls and precipitous cliffs, rice fields, boats on foggy rivers. I also quickly determined that I was the only non-Asian diner in the place, which delighted me, as it indicated that I had made an excellent choice.

Typically, I would have been embarrassed by my blatant aloneness, but on this day I wasn't. In fact, I almost felt emboldened by it. This was partly because I didn't care what a bunch of Asians thought of me, but it was also because I felt as if Dr. Nguyen were sort of there with me, too, vouching for me and keeping me company. I imagined her coming here, maybe after a particularly hard day at Osage Medical and in need of comfort food that reminded her of family, safety, and home.

When a waiter came for my order, I confessed without a bit of apprehensiveness that I had no idea what to order since I'd never eaten Vietnamese food before.

"Could you make a suggestion?" I asked.

He pointed to my menu and said, "Number fifty-seven."

"Okay, number fifty-seven it is." I handed my menu back to him without another glance. "What is it?"

He said something incomprehensible followed by what sounded like "rice noodle soup with half-done beef fillet."

I nodded my approval, and while I waited, I watched what had to be a Vietnamese soap opera on the television above the bar. Standing on a balcony beneath a fake sky of stars, a woman wearing a crown and a man in an ill-fitting tuxedo were upset with each other. Not until someone set a plate before me heaped high with bean sprouts, lime wedges, sliced jalapeño peppers, and what appeared to be cilantro and basil leaves did I look away from the unintelligible drama. Assuming that this assemblage must be the equivalent of the tortilla chips and salsa that come gratis at Tex-Mex restaurants, I nibbled on a few sprouts and leaves while I returned my attention to the soap opera and thought about how horrible it was going to be telling Momma about Dr. Nguyen if things eventually escalated.

"You do realize," she'd say, "that *her* daddy may have been the one who killed *yours*, don't you?"

I couldn't say that I hadn't thought of this, but I also knew how preposterous it was to entertain such a possibility for even a second. Nonetheless, it did make me think of my father, and how his corpse had been moldering in Virginia dirt now for thirty-three years while the Viet Cong bullet that had ended his life as both a husband and a father probably looked very little the worse for wear lying there atop his dust. And not for the first time, by any means, did I think of how different life would have been for me had that bullet missed its mark. Without a doubt, I wouldn't have become the person I became. But who *would* I have become, with a father there to guide me, his sturdy hand on my shoulder, through all of those graceless years of my youth? A man of poise and action, a man of confidence and grit? Maybe.

"Not for eating."

I looked up from my rabbit food. The waiter was pointing at the bean sprouts between my fingers.

"Not for eating," he said again, with a hint of what looked like a smirk on his face. He made one of his hands a bowl and the other a plate. He then emptied the contents of his plate hand into his bowl hand. "For soup. When it comes."

After deciding that ten days was long enough, I called Osage Medical complaining of back pain. When I walked in, I made sure to seem appropriately hunched and aggrieved.

"Dr. Dudek will be seeing you today, Mr. Funk," said the ever-smiling receptionist once I checked in.

My imaginary back pain vanished. "Dr. Dudek? Why?"

"I'm sorry to say that Dr. Nguyen has left the practice."

Hearing this, I felt hollow; the receptionist's words echoed through my emptiness.

"She has?" My voice was too loud in the stillness of the waiting room. "May I ask the reason?"

Still grinning, the receptionist looked at me without saying anything. I could feel her trying to determine whether she should say more. "Well, I believe she's gone back to . . . oh, heck, where was it?"

Wanting to know the truth but fearing it, I remembered the globe that I'd had as a little boy, and how I used to trace my finger across the blue vastness of the Pacific Ocean that separated me from my father. "Vietnam? Did she go back to Vietnam?"

But the receptionist didn't hear me; she had already turned around to call after a nurse who was passing by. "Lindsey! Where was it that Dr. Nguyen said she was going back to?"

Lindsey the nurse disappeared around a corner, but her voice floated back to us: "Some suburb of Dallas. I think maybe it was Ivy."

The receptionist turned back to me and repeated what Lindsey had said as if I hadn't been able to hear for myself.

"Do you know if she has family there?" I pictured Dr. Nguyen's father again, now lying next to a window staring out onto the flat, hot expanse of North Texas with a look of bewilderment on his face, and I cursed myself for having mentioned my mother.

"I don't think so," she said, seemingly unable to stop herself from taunting me with her smile. "No, I'm pretty sure all her family's in California. That's where she's from, I think. At least I'm pretty sure that's what she told me once. Orange County, maybe?"

When she turned around to ask a different nurse passing by whether Dr. Nguyen's family lived in Orange Country, I slipped out.

On my dazed way to Sonic for Momma's burgers and fries, I thought about how funny she would find this, my silly crush—on a Vietnamese doctor, no less—getting smashed so quickly and easily.

"Serves you right for trying to do something like that," she'd say. "And not just to me. Think about your father. He must be rolling in his grave at the thought of his own son lusting after a dirty gook."

She wouldn't limit her comments to that, however. Oh, no. She'd keep on, playing all of her favorite cards: *I don't mean to sound cruel, but let's face it. You're too old to be thinking about romance, and you and I both know it. Besides, what would become of me if you up and got married? Do you honestly think that your new bride—be she yellow, white, black, or purple—would want me around, taking up y'all's precious time and space?*

But Momma, I'd reply, *I didn't want to marry her. I just wanted to take her out to dinner, that's all. I just wanted to talk to her while we shared a bottle of wine in a quiet restaurant. I just wanted to find out who she was. And to tell her who I was.*

Now, why, she'd grunt, *would she want to hear about that?*

I stopped at Que Huong again. This time it was strictly a practical visit; I was hungry, and I'd liked the soup a hell of a lot more than anything Sonic offered. Its clear broth had left me feeling healthy and clean, almost in a medicinal way. Besides, I had nothing to look forward to now but going home—on this night and every subsequent night for who knew how long—to a hateful, blind cripple of a mother and her ceaseless grumbles and complaints.

Once again, I was the only non-Asian in the place. Whether my waiter was the same or not, I couldn't tell. If he was, he certainly didn't recognize me, because when I told him about my first visit, how I'd had a dish recommended to me that I wanted to order again, he just shrugged and shook his head.

"You can't help me out?" I asked. "It was a soup, but I can't remember the number. What would probably get suggested to a guy like me?"

He tapped my open menu, obviously not understanding what I'd just said.

"Do you not speak English?" I asked.

He tapped my menu again and said something that I couldn't understand.

"I realize that I'm the only white guy in here," I muttered, knowing that I was only talking to myself, "but that doesn't mean that you don't need to know English. This is still Houston, Texas, USA, after all."

Without saying a word, he continued to stand next to me, waiting patiently for me to order. I scanned the menu's hundreds of meals, searching for my soup, but all that I kept seeing were the stilted English translations of disgusting things—tripe, tendon, duck fetus—beneath tangled lines of gobbledygook.

"You people eat some gross shit, you know that?" I said.

He smiled, which made me laugh.

I pointed my finger at number ninety-seven so that he could see it. "Bring me this."

With a look of vague uncertainty on his face, he pressed his finger next to mine on the number ninety-seven and said the true, ugly name of what I'd ordered.

"Yes," I said, nodding my head emphatically. "Bring me that."

He bowed, then retreated without taking my menu. I read the name and description of my dinner again: cháo lòng heo (congee with pork intestine and pork blood). Even the so-called English translation was worthless. What the fuck was congee? Whatever it was, mixed with the blood and guts of a pig, I expected it to be just as disgusting as the soup had been delicious. I'd choke it down, though, by God, just to punish myself for my foolishness. In the meantime, I turned my attention to the television above the bar while I tore my chopsticks from their paper wrapper. A woman was walking alone along a beach, crying.

What the hell had I been thinking? I poked the sharp end of a chopstick hard into my palm, leaving an angry, red mark.

Congee turned out to be something that looked like what a large, sick dog might vomit, garnished with a few chopped vegetables floating in its center. I moved my plastic spoon through the thick, grayish mush, looking for what I knew to be hidden within. And there it was: fried chunks of intestines and gelatinous cubes of blood. Despite wanting to suffer for my stupidly hopeful thoughts of seeing Dr. Nguyen outside the walls of Osage Medical, I just couldn't muster the courage to spoon these horrid bits into my mouth, so I made do with the gruel, which tasted about like its color.

All that I couldn't swallow I'd take back home to Momma as a surprise dinner. I'd tell her it was chili from Sonic, and then I'd watch her spoon those hunks of a Vietnamese pig's offal into her blind mouth until I started feeling better.

With the Snow

Jellyheaded from the multiple shots of NyQuil that I had downed to fight whatever it was that was percolating inside me, I found myself growing dangerously hypnotized by the dash-dot-dash of the highway's center line as it shot past. In an effort to bring myself back around, I chewed a palm's worth of Vivarin, then chased down the chalk with drive-thru coffee so hot and bitter that it continued to scream inside me long after I'd let the wind suck the empty cup out the window and into the cold night.

I was on my way to see a girl named Stevie who lived in a pink house on Roe Street in Checotah, to see if she might know where my sister had disappeared to.

While waiting for the caffeine to take effect, the darkness gobbled away at my high beams, the heater blew gentle, warm air against my face, and a young Willie Nelson sang quietly on the radio about time slipping away. And then it started to snow, and the world dropped into nothingness. . . .

I must have been out when that patch of black ice worked its slippery business, but I remember waking up in time to watch the red eyes of the median's guardrail growing larger and wider, winking their worthless warnings, and then there was the gut-punch of impact, broken glass, the sweet smell of gasoline, and a cold wind that made my fillings ache. And Willie, still singing about time.

I managed to push myself through what was left of the windshield, crawl across the crumpled hood, and hop to the ground. Giant snowflakes sifted down upon me as silently and delicately as cigarette ash. Surveying the damage done to what not too long before had been one spiffy red F-150, I was thankful that it wasn't mine. I had slipped into it at the Whip-On-In when I saw the guy who'd driven up in it not bother to take the keys out in his hurry to get beer or smokes or what have you.

Just for the hell of it, I kicked out the surviving headlight with the toe of my boot, which brought the darkness in closer. To keep the snow off my neck, I turned up the collar of my duster and then aimed myself toward what looked like a gas station in the distance. Vibrating with what I knew to be the steady rise of my fever, I hurried toward it as quickly as the soles of my Noconas would allow on the slick white moss growing on the asphalt.

Except for the pumps lined up like shiny headstones and a rusty old truck parked near the dumpster, the lot was empty. As if through a curtain, I stepped from the snowy darkness into a white blaze of dry light that made me squint and wish that I had my sunglasses. The door jingled like some sad Salvation Army Santa when I pushed it open. The warmth inside felt good.

The girl behind the counter woke up and raised her head. "Well, well."

I stomped the snow from my boots and shook it from my hair. "Hey."

"It's been awhile."

I didn't say anything. She obviously knew me, but I didn't know her, although she seemed like somebody I might know. She had that look about her that most of the people I knew at that time had, a look that makes you think of Halloween jack-o'-lanterns, the way they're happy and healthy on the outside, but on the inside, if you peer in through the eyeholes, they're hollowed-out and rotting away.

"Where the hell did you come from, anyway?" She pointed out at the lonely pumps.

"I walked. I had a wreck back there."

She nodded. "You don't remember me, do you? I grew up in Eufaula just like you did."

"You look familiar," I lied. Her name tag said *Lisa*, but that didn't help.

She told me a story about how me and her and several other people whose names I didn't recognize had gotten drunk our senior year and rode the rides at one of those temporary parking lot amusement parks until the cops chased us off for scaring the kids who were there to take the place seriously. I had no recollection of this, but I nodded anyway because I was used to taking other people's word for things I'd done.

"You look like shit, by the way," she said.

"Thanks." I eyed the shelves for something to eat, but everything looked like it would make me puke.

"I'm through here soon if you want to wait around," she said.

"You know a girl named Stevie who lives on Roe Street in Checotah?"

"Stevie Bragg?"

"I don't know her last name. She's supposed to be a friend of my sister's. That's who I'm really looking for. I'm hoping she'll know where I can find her."

"I didn't even know you had a sister."

"I do. Her name's Darcy. She's only fourteen. She kind of disappeared."

"You mean like run away?"

I hoped that's all it was, but I had a feeling it was worse than that. Regardless, I didn't want to get into it. I just wanted to find this Stevie girl, because several people had said that if anyone would know something about Darcy, it would be Stevie in Checotah. "Yeah."

"No prob. We can head on out to Stevie's place just as soon as A. J. gets here."

While I waited, I slept in her truck with her dog, who was waiting, too. The girl had given me her keys so I could keep the heater on. When she came out an hour later, she tossed a pack of smokes in my lap.

"Perk of the trade," she said.

I smoked while we drove through the snow, and then I must have fallen asleep again because she was poking me and saying, "Wake up, we're here." Her dog was panting its hot breath in my face, and the heater was on too high. I stepped out and immediately heaved my guts out, which helped to clear my head. I wiped my boots clean in the snow as we walked toward the crooked pink house on Roe Street. Inside, an old man was eating fried chicken from a box and watching *Cops*.

"Stevie here?" I asked.

The old man hitched a greasy thumb toward the back of the house.

She was there, but she was in no shape to help me out. She was lying on the floor, all sweaty and red. The front of her OU sweatshirt was splattered with puke, which made me wonder if she'd overdosed on something, but there was nothing in the room but a bed, a dresser, an old television, and a plastic flamingo standing in a corner.

"Stevie," I said, but she didn't move. I poked her with a finger, but she still didn't move. I knew she wasn't dead because I could see her breathing, but she was in a bad way. I laid my hand on her forehead. Her skin was cold and clammy like baloney, but beneath that I could feel a fever much worse than mine.

"Damn," Lisa said. "I'd think she's just drunk, but she don't even drink anymore. She's one of those crazy straight-edge girls now."

I walked back to the front room. "What's wrong with her?"

"She's just a little sick with something, that's all," said the old man, not looking away from the television. "She'll sweat it out."

"You her dad?" I asked.

"Maybe I am," he said, and he obviously thought that this was one hell of a funny line because he laughed until he nearly choked on his chicken.

"You think we should take her to the hospital?" Lisa asked me when we were back in Stevie's room.

Since Stevie wasn't a friend of mine, I hadn't yet reached that point in my thinking, but I realized that it was probably a good idea. "Yeah, maybe we should."

With Lisa's help, I hoisted Stevie onto my shoulder and carried her out. She weighed next to nothing. On our way through the front room, the old man stopped us when we told him what we were doing.

"Hold on, now. You can't just waltz in here and take her off like this. She's my goddamned responsibility. Besides, she hates doctors like poison."

I stared into his old eyes for a moment, trying to decide what to do.

Here's what I did: I took Stevie back to her room and laid her on her bed.

"What now?" Lisa asked once we rejoined her dog in her truck.

"I don't know." Already I was regretting my decision to leave Stevie. For just a moment, with her on my shoulder, I'd felt heroic for maybe the first time ever, but that was gone now.

"I always liked you, you know."

I looked at her again, and I wondered if she'd looked like such a toad back in high school. Finally, I said, "Those were the days, weren't they?"

The snow stopped abruptly, as if exhausted.

"Wanna smoke up?" Lisa asked.

I felt too shitty, so I sat there in the truck with her and her dog while she got baked.

Not too much later, the sun began its upward crawl somewhere behind the clouds, and I thought about how everyone else out there in the world was waking up in nice cities and doing things like taking showers and getting dressed and eating bagels with cream cheese and reading the newspaper and kissing the kids and going off to work in nice cars with leather interiors.

Later we tried to get something to eat at a McDonald's drive-thru, but the snow was coming down hard again by this point and she misjudged things and ended up taking out the giant menu with the speaker in the middle of it where the kids inside ask you if you want fries with that, and that's how that particular night finally ended sometime in the middle of the next morning, with the snow still coming down.

I don't remember ever seeing Lisa again, although I might have. I do remember seeing Stevie once after that, though. It was in an auto parts store in Checotah the next winter. She didn't see me, but I saw her. She was standing in line, waiting to buy antifreeze. There were snowflakes on the shoulders of her Sooners jacket. I thought about that night and how me and Lisa had wanted to take her to the hospital but ended up just leaving her lying there because of what the old man had said. I thought about us carrying her and how she had no idea that we'd come into her house and done that. I thought about how I had pressed my hand against her skin in the same way a mother touches the face of her sick little child.

I could've gone up to her and said, "I picked you up and carried you one night when you had no idea I was there, and I almost took you to the hospital, but I didn't, and if you had died then it would've been my fault even if I'd never learned of it."

I watched her go out to her car and drive off, and I wondered if she was still the same as she'd been, however that had been.

To be honest, though, I probably only remember this moment in the auto parts store because of it being tied in my memory to what happened afterwards. No more than fifteen minutes later, in an alley behind the place I was staying at, I found a man stabbed in the neck with a steak knife. One minute he had been smoking a cigarette—I knew this because it was still burning there beside him when I found him—the next minute his life was jetting out across the snow. Who knows who'd done it or why. I was just a guy who'd happened along. Had I gotten there a moment sooner, maybe whatever had happened wouldn't have happened. But I got there when I got there, and he was too far gone to help. All I could do was watch the eyes in his head glass over like a catfish's.

I moved to Muskogee a year later. I haven't encountered anything of the Stevie sort or the knife-in-the-neck sort since—if, that is, you don't count the moment I found out that Darcy had died in a hit-and-run in Tulsa. Every once in awhile, though, I pass through Checotah where Stevie probably still lives, and where the man who got stuck in the neck once lived, and I wonder how exactly the me I was then became the me I became. I still wonder about Stevie, about what she thought when she eventually broke through to the other side of that fever and woke up. Did she sense a difference? Did she at least notice that we'd moved her from the floor to her bed? And I wonder about the man bleeding in the snow. Did he see the flash of the metal as it came at him and know that he was done with living?

And even though I didn't think twice about it at the time, I realize now that the wreck I had that night was one that I'd had no business surviving. At the time it had only been an inconvenience on my way to try to find something out about my sister, but I could've just as easily been thrown into the ditch to die and not be found for days, stiff and snow-shrouded.

Death seemed to be all around me then, but I was only half-aware of it. I don't do the sorts of things I did then, the sorts of things that must have drawn death closer to me, but I feel it more now than I did then, I have to say. I don't know if it's just that I'm older, or if it's come back around to reveal to me the tiny cracks that run through everyone's life, the ones that can split right open without notice and wrench the hell out of everything. Or, just as easily, not split open, I suppose. No matter . . . I'm better prepared than I once was. It's all about caution, I've learned. It's all about watching more and doing less. But does death know I've learned this?

I live south of the Red River now, deep in the heart of Texas. It hardly ever snows here. But when it does, I stay inside and wait for it to stop. It's still beautiful, but not in the way that sunsets are beautiful. Instead, it's beautiful in the way that a hawk is beautiful when it swoops down and snatches a rabbit just so quickly and quietly that you wonder if it would've even happened at all if you hadn't been watching the rabbit in the first place, enjoying the way it was just sitting there so peaceful and oblivious.

A Good Son

Nathan was watching *The Flintstones* on Channel 11 and eating gingersnaps, trying not to think about what might be wrong. He'd just heard his bundle of newspapers thump down onto the sidewalk, followed by the wheeze of the *Ivy Daily News* truck as it rolled down the street. He'd never skipped throwing his route before, but there was no way he could do it today, not when he could barely walk. As delicately as possible, he moved out into the squinting glare to pick up his papers, then carried them around the corner to the gutter on Pecan Avenue, wincing each time that the heavy bundle jarred his leg. It was too hot to be out. The street was dead except for the sparrows hopping in the sprinkler runoff alongside the curb and the cicadas snoring away in the cottonwoods. Down near the fire hydrant, a heat mirage rippled across the asphalt like a shallow creek.

Upon getting out of bed that morning, he'd been struck with a pain in his testicles (and it was, indeed, the word "testicles" that he heard in his head, his father having demanded from very early on that he always use the proper terminology to refer to his body parts) so awful that his knees had nearly folded beneath him. Had he slept wrong and bruised them somehow? He'd gently cupped them in the palm of his hand and lifted them forward so that he could examine them, and they'd looked normal enough, though he didn't quite know what normal ones were supposed to look like, having never seen anybody's other than his own, not even in gym class, since he knew better than to ever let his eyes sink below anyone's chin. He'd never even seen his father's.

Leaden and pulsing, the pain was getting worse now. Already

sweating, he broke the tie on the bundle and began shoving the papers into the gutter's mouth as quickly as he could. After the last *Daily News* disappeared ("Fireworks Are On For The 4th!"), he sat there for a few more minutes, partly to recover from his walk, partly to make sure that nobody rushed out to yell at him.

As he expected, the phone started ringing right after six, which was the time that he was supposed to have his papers delivered by. But since his parents were out with friends of his father's, he didn't have to answer. Imagining his regular complainers—the Beardens, the Hendershots, the Altons—fuming on the other end of the line, he just let it ring while he read *Watership Down* and ate the dinner his mother had left for him. He knew it was a bit babyish for this still to be his favorite book now that he was almost in seventh grade, but he couldn't help it—he loved how the author made rabbits seem so heroic. Soon enough, though, his thoughts drifted from the adventures of Hazel, Fiver, and their friends. What if it was cancer? Or some rare, unbelievably fatal disease that he'd never heard of? He wished he could tell his father, but he knew all too well how that would go: there in the study, his father would look up from whatever ancient book it was that he was reading, his eyes slow to focus on his face, and then after hearing him out, say something like, "You do know I'm not that kind of doctor, right?"

Annoyed that his father still thought that he might believe this, Nathan would say, "I know that."

And then the worst possible thing would happen: his father would make him pull down his shorts so that he could examine him. Them. He imagined watching—and feeling—his father's skinny, chilly fingers lifting and prodding, then hearing him say, "Your mother should take a look." And then without even asking him, his father would call down the hall: "Anita? Can you come here, please?" With his shorts still around his ankles, Nathan would watch his mother come in, and together she and his father would lean in close, talking to each other as if he were not standing there naked in front of them, and he'd hate himself for having tried once again to believe that his father might have any idea what it was like to be a twelve-year-old boy.

Long after his parents had come home and gone to bed, Nathan lay awake staring at the streetlight-striped ceiling, still hurting, still worrying. Inhaling deeply through his nose and exhaling slowly through his mouth, he tried to slow his racing heartbeat, but as soon as he started counting the thumps in his chest, they sped up. Eventually, like most nights that he couldn't sleep, he found himself thinking of Sharla Dusak, who had sat in front of him in English the year before. She wasn't pretty in the way that Marie Brunson or Christine Hunsacker were pretty—she kind of had chipmunk cheeks and she squinted a lot, as if the lights were always too bright—but he liked her hair, especially how he could smell the fruitiness of her shampoo whenever she shook strands of it loose from her shoulders right before taking the daily vocabulary quiz. He also liked how quiet she was in class—unlike the other girls, who all giggled and talked behind Mr. Gelb's back, calling him Nine Toes because everyone knew that he'd chopped off his big toe mowing his yard. What he liked most about her, though, was how she always turned around to talk to him before the bell rang. Although she never said the things he wished she'd say, like, "I hope you're going to Rollerama on Friday night," at least she asked him things like, "Did you do the homework? Wasn't it hard?"

He imagined holding hands with her in the cafeteria, where all the couples held hands. Since she was a gymnast, were they rough and calloused from swinging from things like the uneven bars? He thought about kissing her, too. He hadn't kissed a girl yet, and he frequently wondered when—or if—he'd ever have the guts or the opportunity to do so. Guys like Shane Burch and Vince Fontaine had kissed plenty of girls—and done much more, if you could believe them—and he hated them for it, how far ahead they were in the race that growing up felt like sometimes.

What did a girl's lips feel like—*taste* like—anyway?

To think of her at all was pointless, though; he understood this. After all, he knew how everyone at school saw him—or, more accurately, didn't see him. He only hoped that his father would end up being right, that people like him, like Nathan—"worthwhile people"—reap their rewards later in life, and that those who do well in their youth inevitably fail later, when it truly counts.

"Take me, for instance," his father liked to say. "I'm almost fifty, and I'm so much happier today than I was as a teenager. Living well is the best revenge."

But none of that made it any easier right now—*especially* now, hurting as he was and unsure what to do.

Outside his window a cat yowled—in anger or fear, he couldn't tell—startling him out of his thoughts. He was hungry, he realized. But there was no way that he could get up to eat, not with the misery he was in. Usually he'd go to the kitchen to fix himself a peanut butter sandwich. And sometimes before returning to bed, particularly after a day when his regular complainers had called about not getting papers even though he'd delivered every last one of the fifty-three in his satchel, he'd prank call a few numbers from his subscription list. He knew it was mean—okay, wrong—but he couldn't help it: he liked hearing how scared they sounded once they managed to fumble the phone up to their ear: "Hello? Is anybody there? Hello?" And though he sometimes felt the urge to say something (especially when Mr. Alton, with a quiver in his voice, would ask, "Bobby, is that you?"), he never did; he just let them keep asking questions until they finally gave up and disconnected the line.

He had even called Sharla's house a few times. Her parents' paper was the second-to-the-last that he threw, 124 Bluebonnet. Even though they rarely ever complained about missing delivery, there was something exciting about making a phone near her ring. He imagined Mr. Dusak, who didn't look like he could ever be the father of anyone like Sharla—not with his red beard and orangutan forearm hair—sitting straight up in bed, his angry face glowing in the little bit of moonlight coming through the curtains. "Who the hell is this?" he'd yell, and Nathan would have to fight himself not to hang up, suddenly scared that he could be seen through the line somehow. "Do you know what goddamn time it is?"

The next day was the same as the day before. Once his parents left for work, he pulled on his baggiest shorts and set himself up on his bed (sitting cross-legged worked the best) to read a bit more of *Watership Down*, but because he hadn't woken up to find himself cured as he'd hoped, he was that much more convinced that he had some sort of disease that no one would know about until the autopsy. Then, just as he'd done the day before, as soon as he heard his bundle hit the sidewalk, he dragged his papers around to Pecan, wincing all the way, and stuffed them down the gutter. Unlike the day before, however, his parents would be home when the calls started at six, so there was nothing he could do but hope that nobody but his regulars called.

By the time his parents came through the door, he had already retreated to his bedroom. And at five after six, just as he feared, he heard the phone in the kitchen ring. A few minutes later, he heard it ring again. And then again.

His father, still in the clothes he'd left the house in—gray slacks and a thin, blue short-sleeved dress shirt—knocked and came in, waving a scrap of paper. "You seemed to have missed some people."

Nathan lowered his book. "I didn't miss any, Dad. I delivered them all."

"These three said they didn't get papers yesterday, either. You *have* been throwing your route, haven't you?"

"Of course I have." Nathan said this with as much indignation as he could muster, figuring that chances were good that he wouldn't get many more calls, if any. Other than the Hendershots, Beardens, and Altons—and these had to be the three—hardly any of his customers ever called.

But, then again, it *had* been two days now. And even people who didn't care much about the *Daily News* might notice that.

"You wouldn't lie to me, would you?"

"Come on, Dad." He knew that, unlike some guys whose fathers never trusted them, his father believed him to be a good son who did as he was told, who didn't disobey, who didn't talk back. "Maybe somebody stole them as a joke or something."

His father stared at him over his glasses. Nathan knew to hold his gaze, understanding that he was being given one last opportunity to tell the truth if he hadn't been doing so before. Then his father blinked and said, "Okay. If other people call, I'll just tell them to be sure to check their bushes."

When his father returned after the next phone call a few minutes later, he opened the door without knocking. "Well, that certainly was interesting. It seems that someone called the *Daily News* office to report having seen a boy who sounds quite a bit like you dumping all of his papers down a sewer drain over on Pecan this afternoon."

Nathan didn't look up; he kept his eyes on his book, on the sentence right in the middle of the page: *The sparrows in the plowland were crouching in terror of the kestrel.* As much as he wanted to tell his father the whole truth, to *confide*, he couldn't. He couldn't because his father wasn't Shane Burch's father, who drove an El Camino with gold rims and coached the best Pony League team every year, or Vince Fontaine's father, who kept his collection of *Playboy* magazines on the coffee table. No, *his* father was the father who hadn't taught his son how to throw a football or fix a thrown bicycle chain or handle tools in a way that didn't make him look like a girl or an alien from another planet.

"Nathan? I'm talking to you."

"I guess I'm just sick of being a paperboy, that's all," he lied. Even though he knew it wasn't cool to be a paperboy anymore, he liked rolling his papers baton-hard and throwing them as quickly as he could while peddling full speed, imagining them to be sticks of dynamite ready to blow up his enemies as soon as he was out of range. And he liked having money that didn't come from his parents, though he rarely spent it on anything but fries and Cokes down at the Whataburger on Brazos Street. But since he couldn't tell his father the true reason, this seemed the only way out.

"Well, you certainly made that crystal-clear." His father took off his glasses and rubbed at the red indentations on the bridge of his nose. "I'm at a loss, Nathan. I really am. I guess I was wrong to think you were mature enough for a paper route. I had a route twice the size of yours when I was your age."

The sparrows in the plowland were crouching in terror of the kestrel. Nathan heard the phone ring again. He wondered what a kestrel was.

"What do you suggest we do about this?" his father asked.

Nathan shrugged, thinking, All I know is you're going to feel really bad about all of this when you find out I'm dying.

"Well, I'll *tell* you what we're going to do, then," his father said. "After dinner, I'm going to take you around to your customers' houses so that you can confess to what you've done. And apologize."

Nathan felt a weight—it was like a barbell too heavy to lift—sinking from his stomach to his crotch. But there was no point in protesting. The year before when he'd left a store without paying for a *Doctor Strange* comic book, not only had his father made him take it back and apologize to the manager, he'd made him write a letter to Marvel Comics promising never again to do such a thing. It would be horrible having to do this—he couldn't even imagine how he was going to be able to endure the pain of having to walk so much—but then it would be over, and his lesson would be learned. And then he could just disappear back into his room to die quietly from whatever it was that was killing him.

At his funeral, Sharla would cry, and she'd say, "I always loved him. I was just too afraid to ever tell him." In his will he'd have to leave her something special, something that she'd cherish forever. To his mother, he'd leave pretty much everything else. To his father, he'd leave nothing.

On their way out to the garage after dinner, his father handed him the list of who had called. He counted the names. Eight out of fifty-three wasn't too awful. Of course, the regulars had called in, as had the McKnights on Mockingbird, the Dusaks. . . .

An immediate dampness sprouted across his scalp, and his heart wrenched painfully, as if Mr. Dusak himself had sprung up to poke it with one of his hairy, orangutan fingers. There was no way he could go up to their door. Just no *way*.

No matter how terrible it would be, he'd have to tell his father the truth now.

Nathan lowered himself gingerly into the car's passenger side. "Dad, I've got something to tell you."

His father buckled his seatbelt and started the engine. "Let's hear it."

"I dumped my papers in the gutter because"—he could feel his blood pulsing shamefully in his face—"because my testicles hurt so bad I can barely walk."

His father switched on the air conditioner, then switched it off. He looked over at Nathan, but quickly returned his attention to the air conditioner, which he turned on again. "This is a bit of an embarrassing question to have to ask, and I know I should have talked about this with you before now, but do you masturbate?"

Nathan immediately wished he hadn't said anything. "Come on, Dad. I didn't do anything to myself. I think there's something wrong with me."

His father rolled his window down and adjusted the side mirror. "You don't have to be embarrassed. It's perfectly natural. I was doing it at your age, if that makes you feel any better."

Nathan imagined his father's gray slacks and underwear bunched around his calves, his penis in hand. "But I don't do it."

"You have before, though, right?"

"No." He could tell that his father didn't believe him, but it was the truth; he hadn't. He heard guys joking about it all the time—choking the chicken, beating the meat, slapping the salami—but it just seemed wrong. Gross. And kind of sad. He wanted to save it for when he was with a girl. Wasn't that what he was supposed to do, anyway? Besides, what actually happened when you did it? How much came out? And what if you needed to pee?

"Okay. Well. I can't be absolutely certain, of course . . . and I'm sorry to have to be so graphic, but it sounds like you've probably got what some people like to call 'blue balls.' Which is a misnomer because, well . . . nevermind." He tugged at his ear. "Have you ever heard that term? I think a physician would use the term 'vasocongestion,' if I'm not mistaken."

Nathan shook his head. Had his testicles changed colors without his noticing?

"It's a crude way to describe the pain that sometimes occurs when you get sexually stimulated but don't ejaculate," his father continued, picking at something on the steering wheel. "It's nothing serious, just an excess of blood in your testicles, really, but it does hurt. Once you ejaculate, however, the pain goes away."

Though Nathan hated hearing his father say all these words that he'd never heard come out of his mouth before, he felt better knowing that he might not be suffering from some terrible disease after all. But, then again, there was no guarantee that his father was right; after all, he wasn't a real doctor. If his father *was* right, however, he still had to masturbate, and even thinking about it, particularly after hearing it talked about like it was no big deal, like it was practically the same as brushing your teeth, was so embarrassing that some awful disease almost seemed better. At least then there'd be nothing like *this* going on, this talk of penises and testicles and ejaculation that made him want to get into bed and pull the covers over his head. Instead it would be talk about chemotherapy and radiation and what a hero he was.

His father stared through the windshield at the lowered garage door. "You've had nocturnal emissions, though, right?"

Nocturnal emissions? It sounded like something from *Star*

Wars. He doubted that he could pretend as if he knew what his father meant by this, so he just said, "I don't know."

His father sighed. "Wet dreams. It's when you ejaculate during your sleep. Sometimes you'll wake up while it's happening. Other times you won't, so in the morning you'll find, well, you'll find semen crusted in your underwear." He sighed again and looked over at him.

"I don't think so."

"Well, you'd know, but don't worry. It starts earlier for some, later for others." His father rubbed his jaw as if he were checking to see if he needed to shave. "Okay. Tonight, take some lotion and tissues with you to bed. The lotion is for lubrication. Put it on your hand—you won't chafe yourself that way—and just think about a girl you like. It's perfectly natural. And I think you'll feel better. If you don't, then we'll go from there. Regardless, talk to me in the morning, okay?"

The garage door began to ratchet loudly up its tracks, and the last of the day's brightness flooded in.

It took Nathan a moment to realize what was happening: his father had pressed the Genie opener. "We're still going?"

His father put the car in drive. "I'm sorry you've been in pain, but that doesn't change the fact that you dumped your papers into the sewer two days running. You should've come to me. That's what I'm here for."

As they pulled out of the garage, Nathan hoped to catch sight of a truck careening blindly down the street, dead set on their obliteration.

Uneasily, Nathan watched the Dusaks' street approaching. Somehow he'd survived the first seven houses. To his relief, the Hendershots, Winegartners, and Conroes hadn't been home. Mr. Rivera and Mr. McKnight hadn't seemed to care much, even after he'd confessed to what he'd done. Mrs. Alton, however, had threatened to cancel her subscription, while Mrs. Bearden swore she'd be calling the *Daily*'s editor bright and early in the morning.

His father had convinced both of them that such measures wouldn't be necessary.

They rolled up to 124 Bluebonnet. Though he'd never wanted Sharla to catch him throwing papers (just to be safe, he balled up his satchel and tucked it under his arm every time he pedaled onto her street), he'd always hoped to catch at least a glimpse of her, even if it was just her walking by a window, but he'd never seen anyone other than her father out doing yardwork, shirtless and sunburned. Now he was thankful to see the yard and the windows empty.

"Let's get this last one over with," his father said.

Nathan slowly, painfully, followed. Though he wasn't sure whether he really believed in God or not, he quickly prayed after ringing the doorbell: Please, God, don't let Sharla answer.

When the door opened, there was Sharla, wearing cutoffs and a white Ocean Pacific T-shirt, looking prettier than he'd ever seen her. Her face, much tanner than it had been on the last day of school, creased in confusion. The smell of roasting meat drifted out from behind her. "Nathan? What are *you* doing here?"

Nathan saw her look up at his father behind him. Despite the heat, he felt desperately cold, as if his sweat had frozen. The moment he had so often dreamed of while lying awake had finally come, but it was all wrong. He hated the thought of being rude to her, but he didn't want her to know what was going on, so in the most no-nonsense voice he could manage, he asked, "Is one of your parents home?"

"Ummm . . . yeah, sure." She turned to head back down the hall, but then she stopped. "What do you need them for?"

Behind him, Nathan could feel his father's impatience. "I'm your parents' paperboy."

She smiled now. Her teeth looked extra white against her tanned skin. "You are? Why'd you never tell me? That's so funny."

Here Sharla was, talking to him—outside of school, even—but he didn't want her to be. And his father was behind him, listening to everything. "I don't know. I guess I never thought about it."

When her smile faded, Nathan felt like crying, apologizing.

"I'll go get my dad." She took a step backward, paused, then disappeared around a corner.

"Friend of yours?" his father asked.

Nathan pretended not to hear, though what he wanted to do more than anything right then was to turn around and stab a knife into his father's chest.

When Mr. Dusak came to the door, Sharla, to Nathan's relief, wasn't behind him.

"Hey, bud," Mr. Dusak said, raising the beer bottle in his hand as if he were giving a toast. "You have our missing papers for us?"

Nathan did his best to sound calm. "No, sir, I don't."

"So, you came by for"—Mr. Dusak wagged his head back and forth—"what?"

Wanting to get this over with in a hurry in case Sharla came back, Nathan said, "You didn't get your papers because I dumped all of them in the gutter instead of delivering them and I—"

"Whoa!" Mr. Dusak's laugh burst out from behind his beard. "Jesus Christ, son, don't be so proud of the fact."

Nathan felt his father's hands come down gently on his shoulders. "He came by to apologize."

"Well," Mr. Dusak said, raising his eyebrows, "it sounds like you've got a bit of a problem on your hands, Pop."

"I think we've come to an understanding," his father said, tightening his grip on Nathan's shoulders. "He knows now that he didn't handle things well. He's a good kid, for the most part."

Smiling, Mr. Dusak said, "I don't know about you, but *my* daddy would've blistered my hide for a stunt like that. And if *I* had a son, that's what I'd do, too."

"Well, like I said, I think we've come to an understanding." Nathan could hear his father's voice stiffening slightly. "He knows that he made a bad decision."

"A bad decision, huh?" Mr. Dusak's smile dropped away as if

it had never been there. He took a drink from his beer and then said, "All I know is this: I don't appreciate not getting two papers that I've already paid for. And since you didn't bring my papers, you're doing nothing but wasting my goddamn time."

"Well, now," Nathan's father's said, "I don't think such language is—"

Mr. Dusak slammed the door shut.

Nathan didn't move; he just stared at the door, waiting for his father to step around him and press the doorbell with an angry finger. A couple of long seconds passed. Then when he felt his father's hands lift from his shoulders, he thought that he would see it happen, but it didn't.

"Come on," his father said. "Let's go. He's not worth it. People like that are beyond reason."

Once they were back in the car, Nathan could sense his father's embarrassment quivering in the silence between them.

"See, Dad?" he wanted to say. "That's what you get for making me do this. And for making me look so stupid in front of Sharla." But all he could feel was his own shame. It scalded his skin. How could a father let himself get humiliated like that in front of his own son?

As they pulled away from the curb, he glanced toward the house, mostly to keep his father from seeing his eyes, which he felt rounding with tears, and he thought he saw Sharla watching from a window, peering through a slit in the curtains. Slumping down in his seat, he prayed for Bluebonnet Street to quickly disappear.

At a quarter to midnight, Nathan turned out his light. He had done as his father had suggested: he had brought the Jergens and a roll of toilet paper with him to bed. An hour after hearing the last waking sounds come from his parents' bedroom across the hall, he began rubbing himself, thinking of Sharla. When he felt his penis begin to harden, his imagined hands moved over her breasts as his real hand quickened. He was surprised that not only did it not make him hurt worse, it somehow transformed the pain into something that felt strangely good, though somehow very nearly the same. But then as Sharla pressed harder against him, professing her desperate love, he sensed a second Sharla staring out of a window at him, her silly paperboy with his *daddy*. And she was pointing, laughing.

He stopped.

Outside, a dog nearby erupted into a frenzy of barking, as if a stranger had just stepped into its yard. Furious, Nathan hurled the toilet paper against the wall. Without a sound, it fell to the floor. Were he not in pain, he might have gotten out of bed to call and wake up everyone who had ever complained, but he didn't. The pain was coming back, seeping and settling down again. Hoping just to die in his sleep, he covered his head with his pillow. In the morning his parents would find a cold, stiff body, and for the rest of his life his father would have to live with how he had treated his son on their very last day together.

As he'd done the morning before, Nathan reached down to check himself as soon as he woke up. When his fingers came away sticky, that's when he remembered the dream (but already it was fading), an incredible dream so real that it had been like being awake, but so much better . . . and a girl—it was Sharla, but not quite Sharla, either—naked and lying on her back . . . staring up at him . . . licking her red mouth with her red tongue . . . and he was moving toward her, over her, bigger and stronger than he'd ever felt before. . . .

It was only after he had cleaned himself off in the bathroom sink (the stuff smelled awful—like chlorine, or bleach) that he realized his testicles no longer hurt. Just to be sure, he jogged in place to test them. They were fine, as if they'd never been otherwise. So relieved that his body was back to normal, for a few minutes he did nothing but sit on the lid of the toilet with his eyes shut, savoring his gratefulness.

Feeling stripped clean and new inside, he then ran to the kitchen, raising his knees high with each stride. On the table he found a note from his father: *Give me a call when you get up.* He crumpled it into a tiny ball and threw it at the trash can. It bounced off the side, inches below the mouth. Upon retrieving it, he slammed it in with both hands, nearly toppling the container to the floor.

"There you go, Dad!" he shouted. "There's your call!"

Vigorously pumping his legs, he pedaled through the neighborhood aimlessly, delighting in his ability to do so again, but also thinking about how he wished he could somehow undo what had happened with Sharla. What would someone cool like Shane Burch do? Probably drop by to laugh and brag about how he'd dumped his papers in the gutter, then complain about what a jerk his father had been for making him go around apologizing. If only he could do something like that.

Could he manage something like that? No. He tried to pop a wheelie and nearly lost control of his bike. But why not? He tried another wheelie. This time he did better, riding it along for a few feet. He pedaled harder, loving how he almost felt like a new person now that his pain was gone.

Why not? He let go of the handlebars and counted the houses he passed before he had to grab them again: one, two.

In front of 124 Bluebonnet, he toed down his kickstand. He'd just knock and then see what happened. He'd start by telling her how he'd always thought paper routes were for babies but that his father had made him get one. Hardly able to believe that he was going through with this, he walked up to the house. It was like watching someone going as him for Halloween, someone who could just play the part without having to worry about the consequences, someone who could ring the doorbell and just say whatever, hiding the whole time behind a plastic mask with eyeholes.

Tacked to the door was a note written in loopy, girlish cursive: *Whitney come in! We are in the back!* He ran his fingers over the blue ink, recognizing Sharla's writing. On his way around to the back of the house, passing the curtained window that Sharla had watched him from the night before, he felt his insides flutter at the thought of spying on her. At the fence, he heard a radio and voices. Peeking through two slats, all he could see were a few hanging plants and an empty patio. He backed up a few feet and kept walking. With the sunlight shining through the boards, the backyard presented itself to him a colorful sliver at a time, like a cartoon flip book—grass and rock and water. After finding the widest slit, he stepped forward and peered through it, pressing his face against the rough wood. Mandy Oliver and Christine Hunsacker were floating on inflatable rafts. And sitting on the edge of the deep end, wearing a red bikini with tiny white spots, was Sharla in sunglasses, chipping at her fingernail polish, kicking her feet languidly through the water. Her hair hung twisted like a wet rope down her back.

Inhaling the sharp tang of the pool's water and the coconut scent of suntan lotion, Nathan felt the world around him—the fence against his cheek and palms, the grass beneath his feet—evaporate as he listened to Sharla singing along with the tinny radio: "When the lights . . . go down . . . in the ci-tay." As if he'd raised a spyglass to his eye, Mandy and Christine fell from sight, leaving only Sharla there in the silver shimmer and white glare, rolling the lip of her bikini bottom down to check the tan line along her hipbone. His dream from the night before came back to him, flooding through his body like a pleasantly painful wave of nausea.

Happily, he listened to them talk about going to the mall later, calling Whitney to see what was taking her so long, wishing there were Dr. Peppers in the cooler. When an REO Speedwagon song came on the radio, though, they stopped talking so that Christine could listen to it.

"This was Todd and my's song," she said.

After the last notes of "Keep on Loving You" faded into an ad for Mattress King, Mandy consoled Christine, telling her that Todd was a jerk, and then paddled her raft toward Sharla's side of the pool. "Oh my gosh, I can't believe I forgot! You know what I heard? That Vince Fontaine is moving to California."

Christine sat up so quickly that she nearly fell from her raft. "No!"

"I know," Mandy said. "Isn't that awful? He's such a fox."

Nathan watched Sharla, her skin freckling with the quarters and nickels of light thrown off by the shallow end. She did nothing but continue to push her feet slowly through the water.

"Poor Deanna," said Christine.

"I *know*," Mandy said. "They're so in love."

Sharla stood and walked around to the diving board, leaving wet footprints behind her. Flicking her sunglasses onto the grass, she hung her toes over the edge. "Why can't someone like Vince ever like *me*?"

"Oh, Sharla, stop!" shouted Christine.

"You're *so* much prettier than Deanna," said Mandy.

Sharla hopped once, twice. "The only guys who ever like me are dweebs. It's like I'm a magnet or something."

As Nathan watched Sharla arc high into the air, her arms stretched straight above her head, the haze of his trance fell away and his reason for riding over came back to him with a mocking jab to the ribs. When she vanished into the water, a small splash flowered on the pool's face and then quickly wilted. Before she had the chance to resurface, he pulled his eye away from the slit, his head light. Had he *really* thought he could just come over and talk to her? Had he *really* thought that, deep down, she was probably a lot like him? How ridiculous he now felt for ever having thought it even a possibility.

Before he might hear her mention him as an example, he hurried back to his bike and pedaled away as fast as he could manage, the sweat streaming furiously into his eyes. Gasping for air as he churned his feet, his thoughts screamed at her: I'll get more papers and put the bundle on your porch and soak it with lighter fluid and then light it and ring the doorbell and then run like crazy and when you open the door you won't be able to see anything but a giant ball of fire and you'll scream but no one will be able to help you because the fire will be so big it'll just roll right in, right over you, burning you and your whole goddamn family up until there's nothing left. . . .

Not until he reached the boarded-up 7-11 on Nueces, a street two routes over from his, did he lift his feet from the pedals and let the bike slow itself. He coasted across the empty parking lot until he came to the graffitied side of the building, which faced a weedy field strewn with trash—a tire, a rusted shopping cart, an upended kiddy pool with a jagged hole in its bottom the size of a fist. He let his bike clatter against the bricks beneath the pay phone. Heaving raggedly, he looked at it lying there, its back wheel still spinning, its handlebars twisted around like the broken neck of some pathetic animal. He'd had to spray paint it black because his father had bought him an orange one. An orange bike! Was there a boy anywhere in the world who wanted an orange bike? An orange bike with a white *banana seat*?

It was his father's fault. All of it. Nathan's stomach ached, like he might throw up. Catching his breath, he stripped off his wet shirt and wiped the sweat from his face with the driest part of it. After a moment, he pulled two dimes from his shorts and dropped them into the slot of the pay phone.

"You wanted me to call," he said to his distorted reflection in the phone's chrome. "So I'm calling."

His heart had begun to slow, but now hearing the line ring, it sped up again, bucking and kicking. Relax, he told himself. You're not Nathan Keeble, you're Vince Fontaine.

"Dr. Keeble," said his father into his ear.

Nathan pictured his father sitting in his office, surrounded by books, the blinds drawn to keep out the hot sun. He wanted to say something awful, something that would freeze his father in his chair—his father who thought he knew everything—something that would punish him for having raised Nathan to be who he was rather than who he could have been.

"Hello?" his father asked. "Hello?"

Nathan thought about that awful moment on the Dusaks' porch, that awful, silent moment after the door slammed shut.

"Is anyone there?" his father asked, sounding annoyed now.

Nathan wrapped his sweaty shirt around the mouthpiece to disguise his voice. "You're a coward." And then, believing that maybe nothing could hurt a father as much, even a father such as his, who seemed so oblivious to what he—his very own son—needed, Nathan said, "And your son? He's a loser."

A silent heartbeat of a moment passed. Then another. He could hear classical music playing quietly in the background. A violin trembling.

"My son? What is this? What are you talking about? My *son*?"

Upon hearing how confused and upset his father sounded, Nathan felt the sharpness and anger inside him begin to shrivel, but he couldn't let that happen. "Everyone at school thinks your son is a dweeb."

"Who is this? If this is your idea of a joke, I don't find—"

As soon as Nathan heard his father cut himself off in mid-sentence, he knew what had just happened. A breeze tickled the sweat on his bare chest, chilling him as he watched a small hawk glide silently across the tops of the field's weeds in search of something to snatch away.

"Nathan?" His father's voice was softer now, barely audible. "Nathan, is that *you*?"

Trembling, Nathan hung up. Staring blankly at the phone, almost as if he expected his father to speak to him from it again, he felt the weight of all that had happened over the previous three days come heavily down upon him. He lowered himself to the concrete, leaned against the bricks, and closed his eyes. All he had wanted was not to have cancer and for the pain to go away. All he had wanted was not to have Sharla think he was a loser. All he had wanted was to be left alone.

When he eventually got back onto his bike, he didn't know where he would go, but he couldn't go home. Maybe he'd just keep pedaling until he had no idea where he was or how to find his way back. He'd keep pedaling until it got so dark and late that his father, forgetting everything except that his son was missing, would run to the car and, with his high beams blazing, frantically race off to find him. To rescue him.

Out Here in the Fields (Again)

Cammie asked me to move out on a Tuesday and then I got fired from Lone Star Audio a day later. Or maybe it was the other way around. Either way, you don't have to tell me how pathetic it all was. Regardless, it's the reason I ended up house-sitting for my parents last summer. So I packed a couple of bags and drove across the Metroplex to the old boyhood home in Ivy to bring in the mail and newspaper, feed the cats twice a day, and mow and water the yard while Mom and Dad meandered around New Mexico and Arizona in their RV, collecting crappy Indian pottery and such.

Predictably, Mom had left a note inventorying my duties. *Think of it as a little vacation from things*, she had written at the bottom, beneath the list of chores. *You could use one, I figure.* The note was attached to her ATM card with a second note that said, *For whatever you might need (within reason, of course!). P.S. The PIN is the year of your birthday!*

I felt a bit weird standing there in the empty house. Even though I'd been only twenty minutes away for years, it had been a long time since I'd been anything but a visitor for the occasional meal or holiday get-together. But the cats, Buster and Roy Boy, purring and rubbing figure eights between my legs, didn't seem to think that I didn't belong.

I quickly fell into a routine, though not a particularly productive one. I stayed up late drinking beer, eating takeout from Taco Cabana, and watching baseball. Then I'd go to bed all fuzzy-headed around four, get up sometime after the mail came, put on my trunks, and head out to the pool that Dad had put in a few years before. With the radio on the diving board, I'd float around on a blow-up raft, listening to 97.9, The Zoo. Watching the shadows of the clouds crawl across the turquoise bottom of the pool, I'd drift off to somewhere that wasn't quite sleep but that wasn't where time meant much, either. After I'd pull myself out of the water, my skin hot and tight from the sun now sunk below the fence, I'd dry off on my way inside to drink a few Shiner Bocks, eat a few burritos, and watch the Rangers. Let me tell you, it was nice to forget everything, to do nothing but what felt good.

After a couple of days or so, though, I got a bit bored. The only problem was that I didn't have anything else to do, so I still found myself not doing much of anything. I read a lousy mystery I found on Mom's nightstand, looked up old girlfriends in my high school yearbooks, and occasionally scanned the classifieds for the perfect job that demanded nothing and paid like crazy. Sometimes, though, I'd drive out to our house (the word sounded funny now: "our"), park up the street, and watch for Cammie to come out to do stuff like water the shrubs with our little Clarkie wobbling along behind her on his unsteady legs. She looked good in a way that I hadn't noticed in years, so tan and—well, *svelte* is the word that came to mind, though I'm not sure if it means what I think it does.

Maybe because of how fine Cammie was looking, I started jogging around the neighborhood, which I hadn't really paid much attention to since my Huffy-riding days as a kid. The cottonwood trees were bigger and taller, and their branches now hung out over the streets like they were supposed to in old neighborhoods, like pretty green canopies. The swells in the sidewalk that I had once popped wheelies from were still there, but so were dozens more that hadn't been, pushed up by thickening roots. The Worths appeared to still live on the corner, but the Kinseys and the Bonners were obviously long gone, as were the Depews, whose daughter had given me my first hand job. I ran nine-minute miles, and when I'd round the final corner toward home, I'd sprint until my heart threatened to come apart at the bloody seams. Memories of skinned knees from that very same street came to me as I'd stumble the last few feet, light-headed and side-stitched, to break through my imaginary finishing line, arms raised in mock triumph.

At first, just to torture myself, I guess, I wouldn't set out on my jogs until the brutal Texas sun was at its almighty hottest. Empty except for the occasional driver rolling past so comfortable in his tinted and air-conditioned cocoon, the streets shimmered in their white-hot concreteness as I pounded down them heroically, squinting and sweating. But after awhile I stopped doing that to myself and started running at night instead. Except for the occasional teenager gunning his engine as he sped past me like some blurred ghost from my girl-cruising past, the nighttime streets were just as empty in the old neighborhood as the daytime streets. It was just the angry dogs behind their fences, the sprinklers spraying their jets out too far past their lawns, the cicadas, the crickets, the mosquitoes, the June bugs, the lightning bugs, the moon, and me.

Gradually, my body began to feel pretty decent. I dropped a few pounds, and for the first time in a long time, my blood felt clean as it pumped through my veins. Even my love handles seemed less pronounced when I posed in the mirror. Liking the new me, I actually came to look forward to nightfall.

As I snaked my way up and down the midnight streets and alleys, I saw things. One night I stood outside a house and listened to a couple cursing each other with words that I knew from experience would be difficult, if not impossible, to live down in the morning. Another night I watched as a black dog nearly invisible in the dark tore something small and helpless to pieces. Once, I saw a naked woman just as she drew her curtains shut. I waited around for her to open them again, but she refused to comply.

Still another night I came across a guy shooting baskets in his driveway. I had finished my run and was heaving like an asthmatic, waiting for my heart and breath to return to normal, when I heard in the distance the faint but distinctive whang-whang of a basketball being dribbled on cement and echoing against fences. I followed the sound down the alley to the last house on the street, the house where a friend from my middle school days, Larry Dobbins, had once lived. Under the glow of a bulb rigged high above the backboard, a man around my age was shooting baskets. Even though I hadn't seen him in twenty-plus years, I was pretty sure that this guy wasn't Larry; regardless, he looked familiar. Whoever he was, he hadn't noticed me standing there watching him dribbling and shooting by himself.

Not knowing what else to say, I just said, "Hey."

He froze in mid-shot and turned around. "Hey there."

Squinting from the harsh light of the bulb right above his head, I recognized him then, or at least I thought I could see in him the faint outline of an old self, one without the thinning hair and the extra weight. Giving twenty years of life back to him, I took a guess. "You Kenny Dobbins?"

He clutched the ball to his side. "Yeah?"

I told him my name and that I had been a friend of his little brother's a long time ago.

His face softened. "Well, hell's bells. Lonnie Root! You and Larry were best buds."

"For awhile, yeah. We kind of drifted apart once we got to high school, though." I didn't want to say that once we hit those later years, Larry started hanging out with an uncool crowd—math nerds, band geeks, drama fags—while I somehow came to be partially accepted by those of the campus celebrity set, the ones who drove the best cars and floated carte blanche through school with the smiles of the teachers beaming down on them. "How's Larry doing?"

"Well, he died in a car wreck about seven years ago." Kenny turned and took a shot that rang noisily off the rim.

Larry was such a distant memory that I wasn't as sad as I should've been to hear that he was dead, but I was surprised in that way that we're always surprised when we hear that someone from our past has been dead for years while we've been forging on, oblivious. I told him I was sorry.

"Me too. But it's been a long time, I guess."

When Larry and I had been in seventh grade—that was when we'd hung out together the most—Kenny must have been a senior, which meant that I'd thought he was as cool as anyone could be. He drove a Firebird, for Christ's sake, one with a beautiful golden phoenix emblazoned on the hood for all to admire. He smoked and didn't care if his father saw him. And he had a girlfriend with really big tits who called me Sweetie once. Best of all, though, he could dunk. He only did it once for us, but I never forgot it. He dribbled in full speed from the alley and violently rammed the ball home with his right hand. It was like seeing George Gervin or Darryll Dawkins in the flesh. And when we cheered, he shrugged and pretended like it was no big deal, which made him all the cooler. But now he looked like me: like just some ol' dad.

Kenny tossed me the ball. "You up for a game? I swear, you and Larry used to play all the time."

I hadn't held a basketball in years. It felt strangely good in my hands. I dribbled it a few times, crossing it from left to right, surprised at how natural it still seemed, the movement of arms and wrists, the springy sensation. I pulled up and took a shot. The ball clanged off the rim, but it had felt right coming off my hand, as if only days, not years, had passed since my last jumper. "Why not?"

We established the basic rules—fifteen by ones, straight up, make it/take it, with out-of-bounds being the grass on the left, the fence on the right, and the alley. And just like when I was a kid, it didn't matter who I was or who he was; we just played. And it all came back. Maybe it was what they call muscle memory. Whatever it was, I had it. I juked, stutter-stepped, double-pumped, drove, faded away, and scored. And scored. And scored. And throughout I talked a stream of good-natured trash—*get that weak-ass shit out of here*—as if I had returned to a younger, better version of myself.

But it wasn't like he sucked; he didn't. He stayed with me.

His hands were always just off the ball as I released it, but he never could quite kill it; I was always just that little bit above him, that little bit beyond him. And when he had the ball, he knew how to maneuver and set himself up, but his shots were usually just a bit off, bouncing or rolling off the rim instead of dropping down and through. My defense didn't help things for him, certainly. Just as I'd been taught, I watched his hands and didn't get distracted by movements of the eyes, head, or hips. My fundamentals had always been good: knees bent, back straight, hands out. I stayed centered, never losing my balance.

Over the next few days, between and after games, I learned Kenny's story. I already knew that his mother was dead since Larry had always been known in school as the kid who didn't have a mom, but apparently their father had suffered a heart attack on the golf course a few years after Larry died, which left Kenny the sole survivor. In the meantime, Kenny had married, had a son, and divorced. So when his father died, Kenny had moved back home to take up residence by himself in a house that had once been home to four people. And for the weekends when his son got to stay with him, he'd put up a basketball goal with a swanky acrylic backboard in place of the crummy pressboard one from when he and Larry were kids that had undoubtedly crumbled long ago.

We'd play Horse—I called all sorts of ridiculous shit: hook shots from forty feet, behind-the-back reverse lay-ups using the opposite hand, granny shots with eyes shut, three-sixties followed by one-handers off the backboard—and Twenty-One and Around the World and just regular One-on-One. It was like I was fourteen again. Being fourteen had probably been a lot tougher than I remembered it being, but to trade for those problems now, right? All that I remembered of the summer of my fourteenth year was basketball and riding bikes and playing Galaga down at the arcade and hanging out with Larry and other guys. And wondering whether Kim Metcalfe liked me. And knowing I didn't have the guts to do anything if she did.

Once, after we'd played our last game of the evening, Kenny and I were sitting against the fence, drinking water and trying to get our creaky bodies to recover from playing too young. By this point, we were pretty even. I now had to be more careful not to telegraph my shots. 14–14 games were the worst. Sometimes it would take forever for one of us to make a shot. "Put me out of my misery," one of us would say to the other. "Gotta win by two," the other would say.

"You want to do something tonight?" he asked.

We'd never done anything but play basketball. "Like what?"

"I don't know." He looked embarrassed, like I was some cute girl he was asking out. "Just go to a bar or something. Have a few drinks. Hell, I don't know."

"What the hell. Why not?"

He took me to this hip place downtown that was accessible only from an alley entrance. We squeezed between several beautiful women at the bar and ordered ridiculously priced martinis because that's what everyone was drinking.

"You been here before?" I asked this because we were the only ones in the place wearing jeans.

"Sure." He had to shout to be heard over the Tony Bennett playing at Led Zeppelin volume.

I turned my back to the bar and took a look around. I didn't believe him. Everyone was in black, and most of the guys were smoking cigars. Except for the obvious sugar daddies, we were the oldest in the place.

"Relax." Kenny did his best to smile wolfishly, then finished his martini in that way that implied that another one would soon follow.

"Who's not relaxed?"

A few minutes passed without either of us saying anything. Sinatra was blaring now. Kenny spent the entirety of "Come Fly With Me" trying to get the bartender's attention.

"Are we just going to stand here all night?" he finally asked.

"Quite possibly." I wanted to leave, but I didn't want to say as much.

"I guess it's up to me, then."

I watched him walk up to a sexy blonde. Over his shoulder, I expected to see her bored, blank eyes scan the room for someone to rescue her, so no one was more surprised than me to see her start talking to him as if she actually wanted to. What came next was even more of a shock: not only did she follow him back to me, she brought a friend who was just as gorgeous. Their names were Robin (his) and Marie (mine). If you can believe it, in a matter of only a few minutes, somehow Kenny and I were moving to a table with two beauties who hadn't even been alive when Reagan was president! For the next two hours, Marie and I drank and danced and drank some more and talked a little bit and laughed and then we kissed some and then we all went back to Kenny's place and . . .

I had you going there, didn't I?

Here's what actually happened: because Kenny wanted to stay and make a fool of himself, I called a cab to take me back to the suburbs (for a pretty penny, I might add, but I used Mom's money). And though you probably think I called Cammie when I got home because I'd just seen a glimpse of my lonely future, you're wrong; I didn't. I just went to bed.

Soon after that, I grew tired of playing basketball. Kenny wanted to play every day after he got home from work, but I realized that I needed to get back on track. I didn't really have any idea of what that entailed exactly, but I swore it to myself anyway. So when Kenny came down to see what was up—I'd been meeting him in his driveway at 5:45 for awhile by then—I told him that I didn't think I was going to play basketball anymore.

"I've got to get back on track," I said. The cats were trying to squeeze outside, so I could only open the door a tiny bit.

"What does that mean?" He tried to spin the basketball on his index finger, but it immediately toppled off. "Back on track of what?"

"You know, back on track." I pushed my hands out in front of me in simulation of a train track.

"You're off-track right now?"

"Yeah, I think so."

"And playing basketball is off-track, too?"

"Yeah, I think maybe it is."

He shrugged, turned around, and as I watched him dribble his ball down the sidewalk, I felt good about myself, because understanding that you've got a problem is the first step to getting better, right?

"Let me know if you change your mind," he yelled back.

Two days later, out of the blue, my parents came home. Not only had they not bothered to call to give me a warning, I didn't even hear the garage door go up or them come into the house. Somehow they'd known exactly when to return, because the sight that greeted them was of me doing nothing but lying on the couch with a bag of tortilla chips and a Shiner Bock, watching The Weather Channel. I could've told them how I hadn't been doing this the whole time, that I'd only been doing this for the last few days while trying to figure out how to get back on track, but I knew they wouldn't believe me.

Dad asked me something about my job situation while the weather girl was talking about how it was in the sixties along the Canadian border. In August. What must that be like? So cool that you don't even need to turn on the air conditioner. So cool that you've never known what it's like to start sweating on your way down the sidewalk to pick up the morning newspaper. Heaven. Through the front window, I looked out at the yellowish-brown yard and wondered how long it would take them to notice that I'd forgotten to water it.

I should've left right away, but I didn't. For a few days we pretended that we were all twenty years younger. Mom making me breakfast. Mom doing my laundry. But it didn't last very long.

"What are you going to do?" Mom asked me from the side of the pool.

"About what?" I was floating in the deep end, listening to a Zoo triple-shot of The Who. It had been "Magic Bus" and "My Generation" first, and now it was "Baba O'Riley."

"What do you think, Lonnie?"

"Teenage wasteland," sang Roger Daltrey.

I shrugged. I didn't need to say anything.

"Have you talked to Cammie?"

"Not really, no."

"I hope that you've at least talked to Clark."

I didn't say anything, and she pretended to get distracted briefly by a few weeds in the yard. She'd always known how to effortlessly make me feel like shit.

"You're welcome to stay here as long as you want," she went on, "but—"

"Yeah, I know." And I did know. "I'll do something soon."

"Lonnie—"

I slid off the raft and let myself sink to the bottom. When I looked up, I thought about that movie where a really young Dustin Hoffmann does something almost just like this to escape a party that his parents throw for him. *The Graduate*, that was it. Unlike him, though, I wasn't a twenty-one-year-old virgin afraid of a cougar; I was a thirty-four-year-old father. Above me, I could see the wriggly shape of my mom still standing beside the pool, looking down at the wobbly shape of her chickenshit son.

On what I intended to be the last night that I spent at my parents' house (where I was going to go next I had no idea), I walked down to Kenny's, but he wasn't home, so I got his basketball out of the backyard and started shooting even though it was nearly dark and the bulb above the backboard wasn't on. I set up at what would have been the top of the key and started shooting.

I couldn't buy a basket. Every shot bricked. I started counting my misses: eight, nine, ten in a row . . . and it came back to me how, when I was younger, I used to spend hours dribbling and shooting by myself in our driveway, all the while pretending that, from the second story of the house across the alley, an NBA scout was spying on me through binoculars, reporting my amazing progress to his boss, Dick Motta, the coach of the Dallas Mavericks.

"He's got it," he'd say into his walkie-talkie. "This kid Lonnie's really got it."

It eventually got so dark that I couldn't see anything—not the backboard, not the rim, not even the white net. But I kept shooting, regardless. I'd listen to the sounds the ball made, first against the backboard or the rim, then—a second later—against the concrete, and I'd aim myself toward it, grab it clumsily, take it back to my spot on the driveway and, relying on my memory of where I thought I was in relation to the goal, I'd hoist another shot. . . .

As much as I'd like to leave you with this image of me missing baskets in the dark (it creates a nice symbolic effect, I think), I can't. Before I say more, though, let me ask you a question: Have you come to feel at least a little bit sorry for me? If so, I really do hate to spoil that. Because, what if I told you that instead of getting fired and getting asked to move out, I was the one who instigated it all? What if I told you that it had been me? That I left my wife and quit my job? Would you still be able to look kindly on me? Or would that simple difference make all the difference?

I know what you're thinking now: you're thinking something along the lines of, *What the hell kind of crap is this, anyway*? But everything else is true, I swear to God.

And before you go thinking about Cammie and Clark (and if it makes you feel any better, tell yourself that I went back and everything is just hunky-dory now—maybe it's even true), before you start thinking about how horrible this must have been for them, before you start wondering about all that I've no doubt left out that would incriminate the shit out of me, consider this: I was no happier being the one who left and quit than I would have been if the version I just told you were the truth.

Sometimes *no one* is to blame, right? Sometimes *everyone* suffers, right?

In other words, no matter how it started, in the end, guilty or not, I was still just this schmo missing baskets in a dead friend's older brother's driveway, in the total fucking dark.

The Fading of Whittier

At 7:55, Culver dropped his cigarette in the light dusting of snow and walked into Strick Hall, which, like all the other buildings on campus, had been designated smoke-free years ago. He'd once been able to smoke at the podium as he lectured. Then his office had become the only place he could smoke. After that, he'd been forced outside—like some disobedient pet, he thought. Oh, well. Soon he wouldn't have to worry about such things For his final semester, Culver had requested Tuesday/Thursday upper-division afternoon classes in which he could teach the works of the Fireside Poets, but for the first time since his days as a fledgling assistant professor, he'd been assigned morning classes—Freshman Composition, of all things—that met both Tuesday/Thursday *and* Monday/Wednesday/Friday. It was a slap in the face, but there was no point in complaining. The department's priorities were with the younger faculty, the ones who taught books by authors he'd never heard of and who would rather talk of such fashionable concepts as *deconstruction* and *hermeneutics* than of theme and characterization and symbolism, all of which had apparently become passé at some point. And in their blue jeans and T-shirts, he could hardly distinguish them from the students.

After getting a cup of coffee from the lounge, he walked into Room 121. The click-clack of his heels on the linoleum was the only sound other than the coughing of a student. Once he'd accounted for every name on the roster and every face in the room, he quickly ran through his policies regarding absences, late work, and such—none of which had changed in years—then passed out copies of his syllabus.

"Any questions?" he asked the class.

There were none. There never were anymore. Each semester, the faces of his students seemed to grow more indifferent and alike, like the screens of unplugged televisions. Years ago, universities had only admitted the best and the brightest—students who thrilled at his recitations from John Greenleaf Whittier's *Snow-Bound* on frozen winter days; now they were like supermarkets, letting in all who stepped forward with money in hand. Nevertheless, he turned to the chalkboard and wrote what he'd always written on it the first day of class: *Discuss a book that has influenced your life.*

After running through the same routine the next hour, he took the elevator (one good change the years had brought, he reminded himself) to the mail room to rummage through the tedious memos that had undoubtedly accumulated in his box over the Christmas break. On top of the stack was a note from Dr. Chiles, the chair of the department:

Max,

Driving past your house recently, I happened to notice the FOR SALE sign in your yard. I can't imagine why you would want to sell such a darling house; nevertheless, since you <u>*have*</u> *placed it on the market, I took the liberty of sending out a memo to the faculty, notifying them of this. Due to your house's proximity to campus, I'd love to keep it "in the family," so to speak. I hope you don't mind.*

Sincerely,
Alice Chiles

P.S. Don't be surprised if you hear from Jim Branson soon; he's been hunting for a nice place to set down roots, now that he's stuck forever here in Tulsa!

Although Culver realized it was petty, he'd purposely not

advertised to the department that he was selling the house, which had once bustled with activity, but his daughters had long since grown up and moved away, and now that his wife Janet was gone, struck down the year before by a brain aneurysm, the quiet emptiness had just become too much. In the evenings, he regularly slipped out of his shoes in order to keep his steps from echoing on the hardwood floor.

All of the colleagues he'd ever regarded as friends were now gone—either retired or dead. He had no idea who Jim Branson was. And Dr. Chiles was young enough to be his daughter. He dropped the memo into the trash can sitting next to the recycle bin.

That evening, he skimmed through the responses he'd received to his assignment, vaguely curious to see if anything unusual was happening behind this semester's crop of blank masks. As had been the case for many years, most of the books mentioned belonged either to the group of authors whose names he despondently recognized from the racks next to the cash registers at the grocery store or to the group of authors perennially assigned by the state's high school English teachers. Not that he believed that such novels as *The Adventures of Huckleberry Finn* and *To Kill a Mockingbird* weren't capable of influencing young minds, but he doubted there were any students left in this cynical age who would ever allow anything assigned in school to influence them. Near the bottom of the stack, however, he was pleasantly surprised to find a response that named Cooper's *The Last of the Mohicans.* Unfortunately, it was nullified by the next response, which praised a fraternity's handbook "because it didn't talk only about parties, it talked about tradition."

As Dr. Chiles had predicted, Culver did hear soon from Jim Branson.

"What do you say I swing by your place tomorrow night around seven o'clock and give it a look?" Branson asked, quickly getting to the point. "Before getting in touch with your realtor, you understand. I've seen the outside and just love it." He laughed harshly. "I hope I'm not being too pushy."

You *are* being pushy, Culver thought. But he said, "That's fine."

The next afternoon, Culver cleaned. Since Janet's death, no one but his daughters and their families had been inside the house. It wasn't particularly dirty, but it wasn't as clean as his wife had kept it, and he'd grown accustomed to it looking a certain way when a visitor was expected, so he vacuumed, dusted, mopped, and scrubbed until he felt it was clean enough that Janet would have been satisfied.

At seven, having just finished eating a tuna fish sandwich and an apple, he sat on the couch to wait for Branson. He crossed his legs and lit a cigarette. With the fresh smell of lemon-scented furniture polish in the air, he felt himself return to how it had been not all that long ago. But then the doorbell rang, and the images of china and silverware shining on the dining table and a roast cooking in the oven faded along with the image of Janet standing in the doorway, a hand insouciantly resting on her hip. He opened the door, and Branson, after stomping the snow from the soles of his tennis shoes, stepped from beneath the porch light and through the door with a surprised look on his face, or at least on what Culver could see of it between the fuzzy beard and the brim of the cap pulled down to the lenses of his glasses. Culver knew who Branson was now: the one who taught those courses in film adaptations of literary works, the one whose office always had students sitting anxiously outside its cartoon-papered door.

"God, am *I* embarrassed," Branson said. "For some reason, I had you confused with that guy who offices next to Margaret Eighnhorn, the guy who teaches Chaucer. I thought that was you."

"That would be Carlton Dees." Culver took Branson's coat, a garishly colored thing that felt like plastic in his hands, and hung it on the hall tree.

"Right," Branson said, vigorously nodding his head as he tugged at the sleeves of his sweatshirt. "Of course. I don't know how I got you two mixed up."

"We're both old."

"Oh, please. With so many people in the department to keep up with, and being new like I am, I'm lucky to get anyone's name and face put together right." He pulled at his beard and stared at Culver with such an intense gaze that Culver looked away. "But, to be honest, I'm glad I was wrong. Dees seems a bit on the sour side."

"Let me show you the house," Culver said.

As he led Branson down the hall, he felt upset, not by what Branson had said about Dees (the man *was* sour), but by the fact that this fellow felt comfortable enough to talk to him as if they were old friends, not total strangers. He pointed out the features in each room that he thought were especially nice—the oak floors, the glass doorknobs, the beveled mirror above the bathroom sink, the claw-footed bathtub, the crown molding, the deeply set fireplace, the telephone alcove in the hall. Meanwhile, he tried to ignore or quickly pass by the things that didn't pertain to the house's salability but were, nevertheless, an inseparable part of it to him: the bedrooms of his children that had long ago been transformed into rarely occupied guest rooms, the double bed in which he now slept alone, the utility room where he had found Janet's body lying cold on the floor.

In the kitchen, Culver filled the kettle with water and set it on the stove. He motioned to the chairs at the table. "Would you like some tea?"

Branson sat. "A glass of water would be nice. I still feel a bit dehydrated from this afternoon's racquetball."

Culver handed him a glass of ice water and sat in the chair across from him. He tried not to think about the fact that Branson had chosen the chair Janet had always sat in at meals. No one had sat there since her.

"I couldn't help noticing all the pictures of family on the walls," Branson said.

"Yes." Culver knew that Branson had said this as an opening

for him to speak of his family, but he didn't want to say more. Branson stared at him, obviously waiting for him to continue. "My wife, Janet, loved to have portraits taken of the family." As soon as he heard his wife's name in his ears, something he had not said out loud in a long time, he felt a sense of relief—a lightening, like a breath finally released that he hadn't even realized he'd been holding. He went on: "It was a tradition for us to go to a photography studio once a year, usually around Christmas. If you start with the photographs hanging over the piano and follow them around the living room, down the hall, and into the bedroom, you'll follow us from the year Janet and I were first engaged on through to Christmas two years ago." But no picture from last Christmas, he added to himself. "Our children go from being babies to being mothers with children of their own."

Branson laughed. "My parents divorced when I was four, so except for a few pictures taken when I was a baby, I have virtually no record of us ever being together as a unit." He waved his hand dismissively. "But so what, right? The house is what's important. And I think it's what I'm looking for, especially since it would mean never having to drive to campus."

Culver hated the thought of someone other than himself living within these walls, but having noticed how Branson's fingers had admiringly traced the fading wallpaper, another part of him was pleased that he might have found someone who genuinely appreciated all that he and Janet had worked so hard to establish and maintain.

"If you *were* to buy this house," Culver said, and as he heard the words come out of his mouth, he became aware of his heart beating slightly faster, "do you think you would do anything to it? Anything serious, I mean." Although he knew that it was an unreasonable question to ask, he hated the thought of the house not looking the same, even after he was gone. He quickly lit a cigarette and inhaled deeply. "I suppose what I'm trying to say is, some people like to buy old houses so they can tear things out, build things on, replace original—"

"Oh, no," Branson said, interrupting him. "I have no intention of doing anything like that. Unlike some people, I feel I truly appreciate . . . well, for lack of a better phrase, old things."

The kettle began to whistle. Feeling a little more at ease, Culver crossed the kitchen to fix his tea. On his way back to the table, he tapped ash into the sink and washed it down the drain. Through the window, he pointed at the darkness and told Branson about his garden, how the bulbs of dozens of flowers were lying there in the cold dark, waiting for spring.

The last week of the semester, Culver received a memo in his box from Dr. Chiles:

In honor of the retirement of one of the department's most admired and beloved professors, Dr. Max Culver, a reception is to be held on Friday from three to five o'clock in the faculty lounge. Please come to wish Max well and to partake of the refreshments provided by the last few pennies of this year's party fund!

As he stepped into his final class's final exam, Culver wondered if his students would do anything for him, but as soon as he saw their faces he could tell that they either didn't know he was retiring, or didn't care. Which was fine, he thought. But as the end of class drew near, he realized that he was watching his last students writing the last essays anyone would ever write for him, and he felt this fact as a weight draped across his shoulders. When the final minute ran out, he stood, called for the papers to be turned in, collected them, and then once the last student had hoisted her book bag and left the room, erased the chalkboard and walked out, not letting himself think of anything but holding onto the stack of papers with both hands.

A few minutes after three o'clock, he took the elevator to the lounge. At one point in his career, back when *his* office door had been the one crowded around by students, he had imagined with anticipation the fuss that would be made upon his retirement, but as the time had grown closer, Culver came to wish that his leave-taking would either be forgotten or ignored so that he could simply slip out unobserved. He pushed open the door of the lounge, hoping that only a few people would be inside. Except for a bowl of red punch and a cheese and fruit tray that had been set out on the center table, the room was empty. By the punch bowl was a greeting card. He slit the envelope with his pocketknife. On the front of the card was a black-and-white photograph of what appeared to be a nineteenth-century schoolroom. At the chalkboard stood a severe-looking man in black, holding a ruler. Above his head were printed the words: *OLD TEACHERS NEVER DIE*, and on the inside: *THEY JUST LOSE THEIR CLASS*. Around these words were a dozen or so signatures—most of which he couldn't decipher—and the stock retirement wishes: *We'll miss you! Take care! Have fun!* Someone had written: *Who's left now to teach Whittier and Longfellow?* followed by a smiley face.

Indeed, he thought. Who?

Not knowing what else to do, he poured himself a cup of punch and stood near the window so that he could look out upon the fifth-floor view of the neighborhood. His eyes automatically focused on his house. Even though he knew he was being sentimental, its roof seemed somber now that Branson lived there instead of him. His eyes shifted to the backyard. Were he still living there, he'd have been able to distinguish—although just barely, because of the distance—the purple and orange patches of Siberian irises and Oriental poppies. It appeared that Branson had done nothing with it, although Culver couldn't be entirely certain of this because he had purposely not driven past the house since the day his daughters and their husbands had helped him move all that would fit into his apartment and then divided the rest between themselves. Both had wanted the piano. He forced his eyes away from the garden and in the direction of his new home. It was only six or seven blocks farther north, but he couldn't determine which one of the several nondescript, two-story brick complexes housed his particular unit.

Branson came in wearing a T-shirt that read *Soylent Green Is People!* "So, this is it," he said. "How's it feel?"

Thanks to the intervention of his realtor, Culver had seen Branson only a few times in the past few weeks, and those times had been only in the mailroom or in the hall. Pleasantries had always been exchanged, but not much more than that, which surprised him, because that evening they had shared in January had seemed to hold the promise of—or, at the very least, the *possibility* of—a friendship of sorts. Despite their rather awkward start, they had ended up talking for several hours about all sorts of things—gardening, teaching, literature, politics, history. He hadn't realized how little he had talked to anyone other than students since Janet died. He'd missed it, the sharing of opinions, of ideas. But since then, he'd seen no sign of that night show itself in Branson, so eventually he'd come to decide that he'd simply mistaken Branson's politeness—or simply Branson's desire for the house—for sincere feeling.

"Like the end, I suppose," Culver said.

"Very good." Branson took a slice of cheese from the tray and folded it into his mouth. "How's your new home coming along?"

Culver pictured the apartment, his new "home": the particle-board cabinets, the plastic bathtub, the hollow doors, the view of the parking lot from his bedroom window, the boxes stacked in the living room that he hadn't unpacked. "Fine," he said.

"You know, I've been thinking. I'm having a housewarming party next Saturday. You should come. I owe you, after all. If it weren't for you, I wouldn't even have a house to warm, am I right?"

Culver didn't particularly want anything more to do with Branson now, but he couldn't deny that he was curious to see the house. And maybe, he thought, seeing it furnished with Branson's things would help him forget how sad, empty, and abandoned it had looked the last time he'd seen it. "I'd like that."

"Guess there's no need to give you directions, now is there?"

"No." Culver tried to smile at the joke.

After Branson left, several people came in. The ones Culver didn't know nodded at him, then got themselves cups of punch and platefuls of food. The ones he did know told him how much they were going to miss him, shook his hand, then got in line for food and drink. Dr. Chiles stuck her head in, smiled, waved, promised she'd be in touch soon, and then disappeared. By 4:30, the room was empty, as were the punch bowl and the cheese and fruit tray. Culver waited around for another fifteen minutes, but no one else showed up, so he returned to his office to continue grading.

On his way over to Branson's house (he forced himself to think of it as such) the following Saturday, Culver stopped at a liquor store to buy a bottle of wine. He didn't know whether to buy red or white, so he bought a bottle of each. The first thing he noticed when he parked in front of the house was that the grass wasn't nearly as green as it usually was by mid-May, and he wondered if the weather or Branson were to blame. On the porch he almost pulled out his keys, but then he remembered that the door was no longer his to unlock. He drew his hand from his pocket and pressed the doorbell. The chime sounded different—muffled—from this side of the door. He couldn't remember ever having rung it.

Branson opened the door, then bowed dramatically and swung his arm toward the inside of the house. "Welcome, sir."

"I brought a housewarming gift." Culver raised the bottles of wine. "*Gifts*, to be precise."

"How thoughtful. Thank you." Branson took the bottles. "Don't think the irony of *you* giving *me* housewarming gifts goes unnoticed. I'd have to turn in my professor's badge if I were not to make note of it."

Culver stepped through the door. Several faculty members—he recognized their faces but didn't know their names—smiled and raised their glasses to him in greeting. Despite having tried to prepare himself for the sight of his house furnished and decorated with the possessions of a stranger, now that it was actually before his eyes he felt slightly weak, as if he'd been standing too long. The piano had been replaced by a stack of stereo equipment that was pouring out some sort of unpleasant foreign-sounding music. Movie posters hung in silver frames where the pictures of his family had hung. A glass-and-metal table had taken the place of the upholstered chair that Janet had read in every night after dinner. But the most offensive alteration was the beige carpet that now hid the beautiful hardwood floor.

An Irish setter bounded into the room and tried to leap onto Culver, but Branson snared it by the collar before it could reach him.

"Whoa, boy!" Branson shouted, playfully wrestling with it. "Settle down, you big monster. Not everybody likes to be slobbered on. Let's go ahead and put you out now. Max's suit wouldn't look nearly as good with your fur all over it."

While Branson led the dog away, Culver sat in a black leather chair. Since the conversations around him continued as if he were not there, he looked around the room and tried to see it as if it had always looked like this, but behind Branson's furniture and posters he saw all the things that once had been there, floating like the gauzy afterimage of a photographer's flash.

A young woman squatted next to him. "This used to be *your* house, right?"

"It did."

She smiled. "It's beautiful."

"Thank you," he said, though he didn't know why. "How long have you been in the department?" he asked, just to be polite.

"Oh, I'm just a lowly grad student." She laughed and walked away.

After awhile, Culver wandered into the kitchen, which smelled strongly of unfamiliar spices. The counters were cluttered with dirty dishes. A brown spill of some sort had dried on the floor. Branson was alone.

"Food's almost ready," Branson said, taking up a wooden

spoon from the counter. "Hope going meatless doesn't bother you." Culver watched him as he stirred a mixture of vegetables in a dark orange sauce and, in another pan, bright yellow rice. "You like Indian food? I've been on a real Indian food kick lately. Can't get enough of it." He spooned a dollop of sauce into his mouth. "Yum." He wiped at his beard where a drop had landed, then, to Culver's discomfort, put the spoon back into the sauce. "Have some wine." He waved his hand toward a number of open bottles lined across the counter.

Culver searched amongst the bottles for the Merlot he had brought. He didn't want to drink from someone else's bottle.

"You'll have to make do with this," Branson said, handing him a coffee mug. "I'm out of wine glasses already."

Culver filled the cup and took a drink. He knew there was no real reason for wine to taste differently simply because it was in a cup instead of a glass, but he didn't know how else to explain the strange taste. He and Janet had bought this particular Merlot regularly.

Following the lead of others, once the food was ready, Culver prepared his own plate, and then, because Branson had no dining room table, found a seat in the living room. With his plate balanced on his lap, Culver finished his cup and allowed someone to pour him a second, even though it wasn't from his bottle. He rarely allowed himself more than two drinks in an evening, but tonight the pleasant numbness he felt sinking deep into his muscles seemed more important than self-discipline.

Between bites, Branson and his colleagues talked of nothing but the various goings-on in the department. Culver didn't care to hear about these squabbles and debates—they seemed even more petty and trivial now that he was gone—but he pretended that he did, so he nodded his head and, whenever appropriate, said such things as "Really?" and "Interesting."

"How is it?" Branson asked after awhile, pointing the end of his fork at Culver's plate.

"Very tasty," Culver said, trying to forget the red hair (which, distressfully, he realized could have belonged to either Branson or the Irish setter) he had found in the sauce and surreptitiously removed.

"More? There's lots."

"Thanks, but no. I've had quite enough." In a gesture of satisfaction, Culver patted his stomach, which was now twinging with occasional bursts of fiery pain.

"How about more wine?" Branson lifted the nearest bottle.

Culver shook his head, then proceeded to the kitchen to put away his dishes. A woman whom he recognized as the one who proudly displayed the photographs of lesbian authors on her office door was talking with Dr. Chiles, who asked him how retirement was treating him.

Culver ran water over his plate and fork. "Just fine, thanks."

"I'd do anything to trade places with you." Turning back to the woman next to her, she said, "Wouldn't you?"

"Does the C.E.O. of the Holy See defecate in the timberland?" the woman responded.

Pretending that he hadn't heard this response, Culver reached inside his jacket for his cigarettes. But just as he lit a match, he felt a hand on his arm. He turned to see that Branson had come up behind him.

"I hate to be rude," Branson said, "but, if you don't mind, I'd rather you not smoke."

Culver looked up from the flame hovering near the tip of his cigarette. Branson was smiling, but Culver quickly perceived that it was a smile of cold politeness, not friendliness.

"Not inside, at least," Branson continued, sliding his hand from Culver's arm. "But feel free to step outside, if you'd like."

Culver looked over at Dr. Chiles and the other woman—they had stopped talking and were watching them—then looked back at the match. The movement of Branson's hand had stirred the air and extinguished the flame. An anger welled up in him that surprised him. "I've smoked thousands of cigarettes in this house."

"Well, that may be true, but . . ." He shrugged. "I mean, as it is, I'm going to have to steam off the wallpaper in order to try to get rid of the awful smell that's accumulated over the years, and I don't want to add to it any."

The unlit cigarette hung between Culver lips. He felt unsteady, either from the wine or from the shock of Branson's request, he didn't know. He held onto the edge of the kitchen counter. "You said you weren't going to change anything. That's what you told me that night you came over. Those were the words you used."

"Oh, come on!" Branson's voice was somewhere between a laugh and a shout. "Wallpaper doesn't count."

Noting the embarrassed looks on their faces, Culver stepped backward to allow Dr. Chiles and the other woman to slip past.

"I put up that wallpaper more than thirty years ago," Culver said, and as he did so he remembered that day, how Janet had helped him despite her pregnant belly, how they'd laughed at her ungainliness. "And then there's the carpet."

"Oh, please. It's not like it's shag. It's berber, for Christ's sake."

"And that." Culver pointed at the brown stain in front of the refrigerator. "You're not taking care of anything. It's all just going to fall apart."

Branson opened the patio door. "I don't know what to tell you, Max." He shook his head with a look of disbelief on his face. "I know that this is probably hard for you, but as far as I'm concerned, I've been true to my word. But then again, not everything can stay exactly the same, either, you know?"

Culver knew that if he stepped outside, he'd need to say something to indicate that he was volunteering to do so, not complying with Branson's wish. But all he managed to say was, "You do realize that one cigarette wouldn't make an appreciable difference, don't you?"

"I *do* realize that, but it's the principle of the thing, Max. I don't want *anyone* smoking in my house."

Culver stepped past Branson and through the door without saying anything more.

"When you're finished, we can open that bottle of white, if you want," Branson said. Then the door shut.

Standing on the patio, Culver lit his cigarette with a second match. In the silence, he could hear the crinkle of the tobacco and paper as they caught fire. After he shook out the flame, he took a deep drag and let the smoke out slowly. Immediately he felt himself relax. He walked out into the yard, beyond the reach of the kitchen light shining through the slats of the closed window blinds.

Behind him, he heard footsteps. He turned around, pleased that Branson had decided to come out and apologize. But it wasn't Branson; it was only the dog at the door, trying to get back inside. He walked into the darkness of the yard. In the moonlight, tall weeds cast shadows across the barren patch where his peonies had once grown. Instinctively, he crouched and began pulling them all out. Even though it was much too dry, the soil felt good in his hands. Feeling vaguely tired, yet refreshed, he stood, brushing the dirt from the knees of his trousers, then walked over to where the hose should be, if Branson hadn't gotten rid of it. Knowing that he would have no need for it in an apartment, Culver had left it. It was still there. He turned on the water and pulled the hose with him back to the garden. Maybe, he thought, some of my old bulbs will sprout—despite Branson—if they get some water. He soaked the ground until it was muddy, then returned the hose to its place.

When he looked up again at the light shining from the house, a shadow moved across the window blinds. For a moment it was Janet fixing iced tea for them to sip while they sat in lawn chairs and enjoyed the cool night breeze. After dabbing his head with his handkerchief, he lit another cigarette and, without first shaking it out, tossed the match toward the dry grass near the house. Turning back to the bare garden, he imagined its flame growing in size as it crawled toward Branson's party, but he knew it would die out, that it had already died out.

Welcome

Coatless in the damp January chill, the district managers were just now slinging their bundles of papers onto the beds of their smoking pickups, which meant that everyone, carriers as well as customers, would be getting Monday's paper late. Parrish passed by them without saying anything, knowing that in an hour his complaint line would light up and stay that way until nine, so there'd be no getting any homework done tonight. Inside the warmth of the office, a nondescript shoebox of a building that sat only a few streets over from his high school, the pace was less frantic. Advertising and Editorial were buttoning their coats and clearing out. And now that the papers had arrived from the plant and he had arrived to man the phone, everyone in Circulation was leaving as well.

Taking advantage of the lull, Parrish called Krystal, who he'd been going with for almost four weeks now, but she didn't answer—probably because she felt too rotten, he guessed. According to her friend, Steph, the one with the green hair, she'd skipped school because of cramps. He still felt a little weird about it all—going with her, that is. They didn't have much in common, but she was great. She didn't mind that he drove an old Mercury Monarch with dented doors, and at least once a day she slid a note in his locker that smelled of something exotic, like maybe the incense they sold at Spencer's at the mall. And to think that he'd almost let the stories he'd heard about her stop this before it even started!

The news that she liked him had come from Clay, who had plopped down across from him in the lunchroom five weeks ago, having briefly broken free from Ashley, his girlfriend. "You know Krystal Friel, that New Waver with the spiky hair and all those bracelets? She wants it from you, man."

Both distressed and excited to hear this, Parrish felt a wash of heat shimmer across his scalp. "But isn't she a freshman?"

"So? My father's fifteen years older than the chick he's dating."

"But didn't she get caught under the bleachers last week with Oscar Montoya?"

"Okay, Montoya is gross, but so what? Maybe she's tired of scumbags like him and is looking to get with somebody a little classier now, you know?" He shrugged. "Hell, I don't know. Don't analyze it to death, for once."

Not knowing what to say, or even what to think, Parrish took a long, slow swallow from his Dr. Pepper. He couldn't help it: the thought of being liked by someone who got talked about the way Krystal did frightened him a little. After all, she was one of the ones he'd heard about who sometimes smoked pot in Lance Brandenberg's van before school. And he'd heard that before her dad got sent to jail for something like mail fraud or tax evasion he used to molest her whenever he came home drunk from the strip clubs in East Dallas.

"You're not going to puss out on me here, are you?" Clay massaged his temples aggressively, as if they were causing him intense pain. "God, it's like you want it to be all fireworks and magic and shit. Just get it done already."

Parrish didn't want to hear any more about his virginity, which had become one of Clay's favorite topics ever since he'd lost his own to Ashley the year before. "So, Mr. Big Man, what should I do?"

Clay pulled a brush from his pocket and carefully swept his hair away from his forehead. "Don't sweat it. I'll get the ball rolling."

Five minutes before six, Parrish tried her number again, but she still didn't answer. Was she really not home, or was she hiding?

Five days earlier, when he'd told her that his parents were going out of town for the weekend, she'd given him this look—it was like her face suddenly became nothing but lips and eyes. And then she'd said, "Well, you'll just have to come get me, won't you?"

He'd had a hard time believing she'd meant what it seemed like she'd meant by this, despite what he'd heard about her. She was just so sweet and . . . besides, stories got exaggerated so quickly—even made up entirely—especially about girls. Nevertheless, he'd gratefully accepted Clay's gift of a box of Trojans. He didn't know whether he'd have a reason to use one—or be brave enough to if he did—but later, the way she shivered up against him on the porch while he fumbled through his keys, searching for the one that would let them into the empty house, had certainly made him think that maybe he might.

After sliding her favorite tape, *The Head on the Door* by The Cure, into his parents' cassette deck and turning out the lights, and then after kissing for awhile on the couch, he gradually allowed his hands to roam beyond the safe territory of her back. Meeting with no resistance, his excitement and courage grew. Slipping his hands beneath her Depeche Mode T-shirt—the one with a man swinging a sledgehammer on a mountain—he slid them along the curve of her ribs until they reached the clasp of her bra. Before he even attempted to solve it, however, she stopped him. In the darkness, he heard her bracelets rattle and clink like spilling coins as she moved, and he thought, *just like that, the night's over*, but then she pulled him back toward her and slipped his hands under her shirt again, and he discovered that the bra was now gone.

Though part of him would have been content going no further than this, enjoying what he once thought he might never enjoy, he knew that he couldn't stop now, not if he ever wanted to shut Clay up. Or his own relentless, nagging brain. Psyching himself up, he told himself that he had to at least try. What was the worst that could happen? She might say, "We're going too fast." And how bad would that be, really? But, Jesus, he was scared. Slowly, he moved his left hand down to her sweatpants ("I want to be comfortable," she'd explained when he'd picked her up) until it found the knotted string at her waistband. Before untying it, he paused to give her time to whisper something, but she didn't; her hands stayed where they were, moving in slow circles across his shoulder blades, so he allowed his fingers to go to work. The knot, a double one from the feel of it, was tight, but he kept at it, eventually bringing his right hand down to help, kissing her all the while, hoping that he'd either solve it soon or that she would rescue him.

His fingernails began to ache. And even though she had to know what he was trying to do, she didn't help. He struggled with it for what seemed like several more minutes, but it remained as tight as ever. Not knowing what else to do, he gave up, and pretending as if they had never strayed elsewhere, his hands returned to her breasts. Soon after they did so, however, he felt the heat of her skin cool. She withdrew her hands from under his sweater and sat up.

He could tell now that he'd upset her; she just hadn't wanted to say anything, though had he gotten the knot undone, she would have undoubtedly stopped him then. She turned on the lamp next to the couch, officially killing the mood for good.

"You want something to drink?" he asked, just to disrupt the tender silence.

"What, like beer? I'd love a beer."

"My parents don't really drink." He shrugged. "I meant like water or something."

Stuffing her bra into her purse, she frowned and looked at her watch, which was Day-Glo orange and enormous. "My mom's already going to shit, but if I can get in before twelve, maybe she won't ground me."

As soon as they got into his car, she popped The Cure into his tape deck and turned it up. He didn't say anything as he drove her home, afraid that if he said the wrong thing she might not even wait until Monday to break up with him.

His phone came alive at six, just as he knew it would. He settled into a routine, explaining that it wasn't the carriers' fault, everything was running late due to the printing press breaking down. Saying this got tiring, but it was still better than what the phone crew had to do for three hours every night over at the abandoned desks of the Advertising department. With their crew chief, Gene Gene the Selling Machine, constantly threatening to fire the lot of them if they didn't reach their nightly quota, they had to call numbers out of the phone directory and plead with people to take advantage of this month's special, which was the same every month: four weeks of the *Ivy Daily News* for four bucks and a quarter. A steal, they all swore.

By ten after six, Parrish was answering the phone every half-minute while watching the phone crew dialing away, doing their best to sound excited and sincere. Only Gwen, the newest addition to the crew, had yet to show. Two months earlier she'd replaced a scraggly guy named Asa, who'd gotten caught finishing off a bottle of vodka on break. Five minutes later she ran past him on her way to explain herself to Gene Gene, trailing a cape of cold air and perfume behind her. Parrish watched her hands fluttering about as she talked, but because of the din of desperately friendly voices, he couldn't hear anything. Eventually, though, Gene Gene nodded, and within thirty seconds Gwen was busy dialing away at the last remaining empty desk, her pink coat and furry hat still on. When Gene Gene later walked over to the board to chalk another sale next to his name, she scowled at his back and then, smiling, waved at Parrish.

From her very first night on the crew, Gwen had been so nice to him that he'd immediately felt comfortable with her in a way that he rarely felt with people, especially older people. On her break she had wandered over and started talking to him as if they were already friends, telling him all about her crappy day job at Target, her pain-in-the-ass ex-husband, and her daughter, Pauline, who was in third grade for the second year—all with a smile on her face that seemed to say that life was still pretty good, no matter how much she might complain about it.

"You must be some hotshot, being left in charge like this." She waved an arm over the empty desks of Circulation.

He laughed, though he was proud of how much Mr. Royal, the Circulation Manager, trusted him. "All I do is answer phones."

"Now, now." She wagged a finger at him. "Don't be modest. Next thing you'll be telling me is you don't have to beat the girls off with a stick."

Not yet knowing that Krystal Friel liked him, he rolled his eyes at this. He'd kissed a grand total of two girls in his life so far, and one had been Lisa Epps, who everyone called Moon Dog. "In my dreams."

"I swear, girls never know who the right guys are until it's too late. I sure didn't. I was only interested in the ones who liked dragging Fifteenth Street and getting into fights. That's how I ended up leaving school with a daughter instead of a diploma." Cocking her thumb, she shot a finger at her temple. "All I hope is that Pauline runs with a better crowd than I did when she gets older because, unlike her mother, she's going to be pretty, and pretty spells nothing but trouble."

Though he felt embarrassed by her openness, he also knew that it would be rude to let such a comment slide without making an objection. "Come on, now. You're very attractive."

Feeling his cheeks redden, Parrish wondered whether he believed what he'd just said. It was hard for him to know because, when he looked closely at her, he saw someone more like his parents than himself. She'd probably been pretty when she was his age, he guessed, but now her face, especially her eyes, looked tired in a way that more sleep probably wouldn't help much.

She rested her hand on his arm. "Well, it's sure sweet of you to say so, anyway."

Parrish took his last call at nine o' clock, the same time that the phone crew began gathering their stuff and filing out, groaning and laughing. As usual, Gwen hung back, bringing up the rear.

"Two whole sales tonight," she said to Parrish, who was moving through the office flipping off the lights. "Pretty soon Gene Gene'll fire the rest of the crew and just keep me, I'm bringing in so many subscriptions, you know?"

"Gene Gene's all talk. He never fires anybody. Except that guy before you."

Outside, Parrish locked the door behind them. A loose page of the *Daily News* drifted and dragged across the pavement as they walked toward their cars.

Gwen turned her back to the wind so that she could light a cigarette. "You headed to your girlfriend's?"

Hearing Krystal mentioned, he realized how little he'd thought about her over the last few busy hours, which was a big change from the day before, when he'd nearly been incapacitated by worry, fearing that he'd pushed her too far on Saturday night. Having hung up several times before letting himself press the last button of her number, he'd finally called. Though she hadn't had time to talk (she was helping her mom in the kitchen, she'd said), he'd been relieved to hear her sound like her normal self upon recognizing his voice. Everything seemed okay—Saturday night hadn't been the disaster he'd feared.

"I don't know, maybe," Parrish said, even though Krystal's mother wouldn't let anyone come over after nine during the week. Regardless, it felt good to act so nonchalant, as if Krystal were waiting around for him, hoping that he might drop by.

"Wish *I* had somewhere fun to go," Gwen said, unlocking her car. "Oh, well. Don't do anything I wouldn't do, sweetie."

Shivering on the cold vinyl seat, Parrish watched Gwen's taillights disappear onto Brazos Avenue. It wasn't until he turned on the headlights that he noticed the square of folded paper tucked under his windshield wiper.

Lying on Clay's bed twenty minutes later, his face scrubbed clean of tears, Parrish read Clay the note. Though she didn't say as much—she only said things like *It has nothing to do with you really* and *I'm sorry* and *You're sweet*—he'd been right about having tried to go too far on Saturday, just as he'd feared.

When he finished, Clay said, "Well, that's a hell of a lot nicer than what she's been telling everyone else, that's for sure."

"What do you mean? You already knew she was breaking up with me?"

Clay was standing shirtless in front of his mirror, a dumbbell in each hand, staring intently at his muscles. "Ashley told me an hour ago."

"How would she know anything about it?" Parrish asked, angry that his night with Krystal was already the subject of gossip.

"You know how girls talk. That's all they fucking *do*, practically. Whoever drove Krystal up to your work told her, I guess. But who cares how she heard? What you should be worrying about is that Krystal's going around saying that you were too scared to fuck her."

The blood thrumming hot in his face cooled, then seemed to drain away, not only out of his head but out of his body. He felt sick. Numb. He tried to imagine Krystal saying something this awful, but he couldn't do it. "She did not."

Clay pointed to his phone. "Hey, call Ash yourself if you don't believe me."

Even though he hadn't wanted to tell Clay what had happened Saturday because he didn't want to hear the inevitable review of his mistakes, Parrish now knew he had to defend himself, so he described the trouble he'd had with the knot of Krystal's sweatpants, how long he'd worked at it in his effort to get it undone. "She *had* to know I was trying, but I just couldn't get it. She should have helped—"

"Oh, come on!" Clay dropped his dumbbells onto the bed, where they bounced and clanked together, then rolled heavily against Parrish's thigh. "A girl may help you with getting her bra off, but she's not going to take her fucking *pants* off for you; don't you understand that? Not even a little nympho like that. You've got to take control! That's what they *want* you to do! You should've gotten some scissors and cut that fucking thing in half, you know what I'm saying?"

"You're right. Maybe I should have just raped her." Parrish wished now that he'd driven home and gone to bed.

"Would you shut the fuck up? Girls aren't little angels. They know the score. Especially *that* girl." He grabbed a shirt from the floor and wiped the sweat from his chest. "She is a fucking bitch, though, talking shit like that. But, man, Parry, what am I supposed to think, huh? I mean, seriously."

The phone rang. And while Clay talked—it was Ashley—Parrish walked out to his car. Resting his head against the cold steering wheel, he closed his eyes and saw the dark lipstick of Krystal's mouth, which he wanted to kiss again. And break his hand against, too. To punish himself, he popped in Krystal's tape, which she'd forgotten in her rush to get inside before midnight. After fast-forwarding it to her favorite song, which he only now wretchedly realized began with the line, *Say goodbye on a night like this if it's the last thing we ever do*, he turned it up so loud that his lousy speakers threatened to burst from their sockets.

At school, Parrish slunk listlessly from class to class, fearing that any moment someone would stop him to ask if the story going around was true. Only once did he see Krystal. Before stepping into Mr. Wood's room for government, he allowed himself to watch her for a moment, though he was careful not to let her see him. Down at the other end of the hall she was in a tight huddle with Steph and a few of her other friends. Their garish hair occasionally flashed and bobbed into view between the heads and shoulders of students ambling toward the science hall—and even amidst the between-period noise, he could hear them cackling and shrieking. He wished that he didn't know what they were talking about.

And only once did he see Clay, who didn't even acknowledge

him with the usual cool lift of the head as he strolled by with Ashley tucked under his arm.

At work that night, to keep from having to walk out with Gwen after turning out the lights, he ducked into the restroom five minutes before nine. He stood waiting in front of the mirror, watching himself breathing and blinking. Not until he couldn't hear anything but the hum of the copier did he step back into the fluorescent emptiness of the office.

Outside, Gwen's car was idling beside his in a cloud of exhaust lit red by her taillights. When he drew close, she opened her door.

"I was about to head on home," she said, "but then I decided to stick around since we didn't get to talk. So what's up?"

Parrish opened his mouth to say, "Nothing," but nothing came out. He felt his face betraying him.

"It's not that girlfriend of yours, is it?"

An ache swelled through the muscles of his jaw as he nodded, and then, hating himself for being so weak, he felt his eyes blur the slightest bit.

"You poor thing. Come sit in here with me for a sec." She leaned over and popped the passenger door open.

Parrish swiped at his eyes with the sleeve of his coat. Inside, it was warm and smoky and dark. The only light came from the dashboard console's green glow. "She broke up with me last night."

"Oh, that little bitch." Cigarette smoke drifted from Gwen's mouth, a slow, green-illumined cloud. She patted his hand. "Talk to me. I'm in no hurry whatsoever to get home because Pauline's at her worthless daddy's tonight. It won't change a damn thing, but it'll make you feel better to get it off your chest. I can see it built all up inside you."

He intended only to tell her that Krystal hadn't even had the guts to break up with him face-to-face, but he kept on, telling Gwen how much he'd liked her, how confused he was by everything. And though he didn't elaborate with any of the embarrassing details, he felt she would have understood.

By the time he finally stopped, he felt drained, as if he'd been talking uninterrupted for half an hour. "It must all sound pretty silly to you, I guess."

She laughed. "Just because I'm older than you doesn't mean things like that change all that much."

For a moment, the only sound was the quiet rush of the heater and the low burble of the idling engine. Embarrassed suddenly, Parrish now regretted having said anything. "I should get going so you can go home. Besides, I've got school in the morning, so—"

She ground her cigarette out in the ashtray between them. "School schmool. You work too hard, you know that? Cut yourself some slack now and again. Don't waste these years acting like an adult before you have to."

He knew she was thinking about her own tough teenage years, and he tried to imagine himself in a similar situation—Krystal big and pregnant with his child—but he couldn't do it; all he could see was his virginity stretched for miles before him in all directions, like a cornfield that he'd never find his way out of.

She lit another cigarette. "Why don't you come over for awhile? The last thing you need is to be sitting around stewing in your own juices."

Parrish couldn't make out her expression in the dark. She wasn't propositioning him, was she? He felt flattered, but a little sickened, too—maybe more sickened than flattered. She was an *adult*. She had a *child*. "I don't know, Gwen. I don't think so."

Gwen laughed, then poked a finger into his ribs. "You're a riot. You really are."

He rubbed his eyes. Okay, so she just felt sorry for him. That was more understandable.

"Come on, just for awhile." She poked him again. "Geez, you're so uptight! It's like you're wearing a three-piece suit all the time."

Whatever her reason for asking him over, he was tired of

hearing this sort of thing. "Okay. Just for awhile."

He followed her car as she turned onto Neches, a street he couldn't remember ever driving down before. She pulled into the lot of an apartment complex that looked as if it might have once been a motel. He parked a few spaces down from her, next to a purple Monte Carlo with a large sticker of the Virgin Mary on its rear window, and then followed her up the stairs. It was so different now that they weren't at work. He felt strangely exposed, like a turtle pulled from its shell.

"Well, here we are." She unlocked the door and pushed it open. "It's not much, but I call it a dump."

The living room, which smelled like the potpourri his mother liked to put out before guests came over, was small—there wasn't much space between the couch and the coffee table or the coffee table and the television—but neat. The carpet was still ribbed with the tracks of a recent vacuuming. "It's nice."

"It beats living on the street." She turned on the television on her way into the kitchen. "Thirsty? You can have some wine with me just as long as you don't tell anybody I go around contributing to the delinquency of minors."

Parrish sank into the tired softness of the couch. He hadn't liked how wine tasted the few times his parents had let him have it. "No, thanks."

Gwen came back in with a bottle of red wine and two glasses. "You sure? There's nothing wrong with a glass now and then, you know. It's good for the blood. And it's relaxing. Damned relaxing." After sitting next to him, she set the glasses on the coffee table and filled them both.

Actually, he wasn't sure. Despite his reason for refusing, he wasn't sure that he didn't want to just say *Screw it* and do something for the hell of it, even something he didn't particularly want to do. But he still had to drive home, and there was no way he could take the chance of getting pulled over with alcohol on his breath. And now that he thought of it, because he'd been so focused on keeping up with her Pontiac, he wasn't even sure how to find his way out of this neighborhood and back home.

"You sure you don't want just a smidge?" Gwen asked.

To hell with it, he said to himself with as much conviction as he could muster. To hell with it. What do I care? Krystal broke up with me. To hell with it. He picked up the glass filled less high and raised it to his lips.

For the third time now, Mick Jagger was singing about neighbors.

Watching wine sloshing from Gwen's glass as she danced around the living room, Parrish wondered about her daughter as he took the first sip of his second glass. What was it like to have a mother like this, one who asked high school guys over to hang out and drink? Did she do this sort of stuff all the time? It didn't seem likely, but maybe so. Smiling, she approached him with her hand out. Her teeth were slightly purple.

"Get on your feets, mister," she said.

Not until Krystal had he ever danced with anyone. At the last school dance, they'd held on to each other while the deejay played "I Melt With You" by Modern English, the only song she'd requested that the deejay had. With her humid body pressed snugly against his, Parrish had wanted it to never end. "I don't think so, Gwen."

"God, you're just so awfully *mature* all the time," she said in an exaggerated British accent. She grabbed the collar of his shirt and pulled. "Come on, live a little."

"No, really." Feeling muffled by the wine, he strained against her grip, suddenly nervous that he might not be able to keep himself from being pulled off the couch. "I don't want to. Really."

She let go of him, then went over to the turntable and shut the music off with a brusque snap, making the needle skitter and pop before coming to rest in the middle of one of Mick's slowly dying yowls. When she dropped down next to him, he feigned interest in the black-and-white movie on the TV even though the sound was off. A woman with an ankle bracelet was slowly walking down some stairs. He snuck a glance over at Gwen; she was looking at him. Her face was serious, blank, as if not only had she not just been dancing and laughing, but that she hadn't danced or laughed in years. But then she smiled and shook her head in that way he knew meant that he was supposed to ask her what was so funny, but he didn't want to.

"You're not the only one with problems, you know," Gwen said.

"I never said I was."

"I got the 'I'm going to have to let you go if you don't shape up' speech tonight from Gene Gene. If I don't make twenty sales by Friday, I'm gone." She took the glass from his hand and guzzled what was left in it. "Like that's going to happen." She poured more wine into both glasses. "I wasn't going to say anything since you were so upset, but . . ." She wiped at her eyes. "I've got as much chance of getting twenty as I've got of getting a hundred, so what's the point, you know? I might as well start looking for another shitty second job."

"I'm sorry." He didn't know what else to say, so he just repeated himself. "I'm really, really sorry."

"Forget it." When she looked over at him, her face looked different, almost as if she barely recognized him. "It's getting late. You've got better things to do than to hang out with an old lady, anyway. I was just trying to make you feel better, is all. But I guess I didn't do a very good job of that, either."

Parrish turned his eyes back to the television so as not to have to look at her. "Come on, you're not an old lady. You're just tired. And you've had quite a bit to drink, too."

She laughed, but there was no pleasure in it. "Welcome to my world, sweetie. By the end of the day, I'm too tired to do anything but drink booze and watch TV, even though there's always something that needs doing. Laundry. Dishes. Bills that I can't pay because of what I have to spend on sitters when my mom can't keep Pauline. And that's my life, every single day. I don't talk to anyone but customers wanting to know what aisle the ironing boards are on, and at night it's people pissed off that I've called and interrupted their relaxing evening. It just gets exhausting. And now . . ." Her voice quavered. "And now . . ."

Instinctively, Parrish put his arm across her shoulders as she began to cry. He intended only to keep it there for a second, but before he could move, she sank toward him, dripping tears.

Before the week was over, Parrish could see it in the faces that drifted past him in the halls: word of his night with Krystal had spread, even amongst the people he didn't know. No one said anything, but he could tell what they were thinking. And if they didn't believe it now—that he was "scared of pussy," as he'd heard that Krystal, being cruder than he could ever imagine her being, was going around saying, then he knew they'd believe it soon enough simply from hearing it repeated, passed on, embellished.

Over the next few months, whenever he saw Krystal in the halls he pretended not to know her, and he was grateful that she did the same. He still had her *Head on the Door* cassette, and occasionally he considered pulling out the tape and stringing it like Christmas garland across her locker, particularly whenever he saw her striding down the hall in Ryan Littlejohn's too-big FFA jacket, but she'd know who was responsible. Besides, her new look—starched Wranglers and red Justin Ropers—probably meant that she'd already abandoned The Cure for Alabama and George Strait anyway.

As he trudged on through the year, he tried not to think too much about what the story of that night had become, but it was hopeless; he'd heard that even Clay was talking about him behind his back—Clay, who hadn't talked to him since the awful night of Krystal's note. At work, though, he was thankful to escape the troubles of school. Though he kept hoping that Gwen would call in on the complaint line, she never did, just like she'd never come back to the phone crew after that night at her apartment. When she'd stopped crying, they'd sat in silence together, just watching the movie with the sound off. And in that silence, his arm still around her shoulders, he'd thought about what a pussy Clay would have said he was being. *What are you waiting for?* he would have asked. *A fucking written invitation?*

"Parry. Hold on."

Though years would pass—he would graduate from college, fall in love, get married, have children—he would still occasionally hear these words again, usually late at night while lying sleepless in bed, his thoughts having segued from the events of his day to the deeds of his life. He remembered leaning close and kissing Gwen's neck, curling his hand over her jeaned thigh. Next to his sleeping wife, he would convince himself that, yes, most definitely, he'd been attracted to her at that moment, and he knew that he'd always really, genuinely, liked her, so why had he then said what he did when she pulled away—and this she'd done gently, too, not at all harshly—and whispered what she had? He realized later that Gwen might have merely meant for him to pause a second, to hold on while she shifted into a more comfortable position or something, but at the time he heard it only as a plea to stop. He heard it distinctly as a rejection, a hand raised like a red sign. But even so, even if she *had* wanted him to stop, why had he leapt to his feet and said what he did?

Why the fuck did you invite me over, then?

Watching these words strike her almost physically there in the epileptic light thrown off by the television, he hadn't stopped. With his jaw clenched so tightly the words hardly had space to escape his mouth, he roared on, letting loose with an anger that, even in the midst of it, he knew had nothing to do with her. And then he left, storming down the stairs so violently that the heels of his shoes rang like gunshots against the metal steps.

Several months later, on a Saturday in August, just a few days before the beginning of his senior year, Parrish ran into Gwen at the Stop-N-Go on Sam Houston.

"Well, well," she said with a smile, though only a small one. "Look what the cat dragged in."

Caught by surprise, and having no other option since he had to pay for the gas he'd just put in the Monarch, he stepped into line behind her, aflame with embarrassment. Dozens of times he'd thought about driving by her apartment some night after work—if he could find it again, that is (he still didn't know how he'd found his way home that night)—but he'd always talked himself out of it before getting very far down Brazos. Immediately he noticed that she looked happier and healthier than he ever remembered her looking. "Me, I guess."

She raised a bag of Tostitos and a six-pack of Sprite. "Pauline and her friends needed some snacks. My mother's holding down the fort."

A few quiet seconds passed between them while ZZ Top buzzed from a speaker in the ceiling. He felt a desperate urge to immediately apologize, to *finally* apologize—before he'd even left her parking lot that night he'd felt rotten, terrible—but he couldn't get himself to say anything, not with all the people standing around. What would the two guys buying motor oil and Coors behind him think if they heard him say what he might end up saying?

"Still at Target?" he asked.

She laughed. "No, thank the good Lord. I've got an honest to goodness *job* now, if you can believe it. I'm an administrative assistant at a place out in Rowlett. It's just a fancy way of saying that I'm a secretary, but I'm not complaining. You still at the paper?"

"Yeah." He was about to add that Gene Gene had been fired for turning in subscriptions for people whose names he'd gotten from the obituaries, but it was her turn now to get rung up. She asked the clerk for a carton of Virginia Slims, paid, and then walked toward the exit. Watching her pass the displays of Dr. Pepper and Fritos, he expected her to wait for him at the door, but when she didn't, when she just pushed through and stepped outside as if she hadn't run into him at all, he had to fight the urge to shout her name across the store as he fumbled to open his wallet. After paying, he rushed out into the sickening heat, nearly knocking over a rack of magazines, hoping to catch her. He couldn't let her disappear like this. Upon seeing her Pontiac just about to swing onto the street, he whistled and waved his arms.

Running past the pumps now, he yelled, "Gwen! Stop!"

When her reverse lights flashed on, he slowed, relieved, knowing that she had seen him. By the time he reached her, her passenger door was open.

Nearly breathless, he climbed in. "Thanks."

She backed up into a space next to the pay phones but left the engine on and the air conditioner running. The deejay on the radio said that he'd be back with a triple-shot of Stevie Ray Vaughn. "I think you nearly gave that old guy in the Cadillac a heart attack, running out yelling like that."

He felt his own heart still beating hard. "I just wanted to make sure I got your attention."

She broke open the cigarette carton. "Well, you got it."

He hoped she'd say something else, something to ease the tension—even if it was nothing more than *So, what's up?*—but she didn't. He had no reason now not to be able to bring it up, no reason not to say what he wanted to say, but he couldn't get himself to open his mouth. He listened to her tear the cellophane from a pack, but he didn't turn to look her way. Watching the cars speeding past in hot sparkles of metal and white bursts of glass, he wished he were back in the Monarch and out amongst them, weaving his way down Sam Houston toward home. He heard the rasp of her lighter, the inhalation of her breath, and then he smelled the first cloud of smoke.

"I'm not mad at you, you know," she said. "Not anymore, at least."

Hearing this, Parrish felt his throat tighten as if someone in the backseat had risen up and put him in a chokehold. "I'm sorry, Gwen. I really am."

With smoke pluming from her mouth, she said, "I know you are."

"I didn't mean what I said. I was just upset."

"I know you were, you little shit." She reached over and patted his knee. "We just were both in a bad way that night, I guess."

The words came in a rush then. He told her what had really happened with Krystal, how he'd been abandoned by his best friend, how he now felt so lost and angry. It felt so good spilling out—the poison, the hate, the isolation, the misery.

"And you know what?" he said, feeling again as he'd felt with Gwen before all of this. "I sent a note to the principal that said that Krystal was selling pot in the east wing bathroom after second period." For a second, her laugh drowned out Stevie Ray's guitar. Hearing it made him so happy that, as he continued, he laughed, too. "I cut letters out of the *Daily News* so they wouldn't recognize my handwriting. You know, like a ransom note. I don't think anything ever happened to her, though."

"Don't you worry," Gwen said, the cool flatness of her voice from earlier now gone. "She'll get her comeuppance one of these days." She blew smoke against the windshield. "Just you wait."

Even though he imagined that the Stop-N-Go clerk had to be wondering where the driver of the Monarch still sitting at Pump #4 had disappeared to, Parrish didn't want to leave yet. He liked being with her again after all of these months, but he didn't know what else there was for him to say; he felt emptied out now, nearly hollow. Stevie Ray was singing about the weather, how he couldn't stand it. Seconds were ticking by. He put his hand on the door handle. "Well . . ."

"You want to come over for a bit? I'm in a new place over on Sabine. It's a hell of a lot nicer than the place I was in before." She flattened what was left of her cigarette into the ashtray. "I'd like you to meet my daughter."

Through the windshield he watched a mockingbird hopping across her hood with something plastic in its mouth. "Sure. I'd like to."

Following her over, he tuned his radio to the station Gwen

had been listening to, liking the thought that they were listening to the same thing at the same time.

As soon as they stepped through the door, one of the four young girls sprawled across the couch in front of the television said, "Grandma's taking a nap. Did you remember the Funyuns?"

"They didn't have any," Gwen said, raising the bag of Tostitos, "so I got these."

The girl moaned. "I *hate* Tostitos."

"My lovely daughter," Gwen said to Parrish. To her daughter, she said, "Pauline, I'd like you to meet Parry. He's a friend of mine."

"It's nice to meet you," Parrish said.

Pauline grunted, not glancing away from the television.

"Oh, well," he said to Gwen with a smile, shrugging.

Gwen laughed. "Exactly. Welcome to the world of the invisible."

A few minutes later, Parrish would be heading back downstairs to his car, but for the moment he was enjoying how nice it felt standing there quietly next to Gwen, watching the girls watching cartoons. Not caring whether Pauline saw or not, he reached over and took Gwen's hand and squeezed it. When she squeezed back, he held on, already regretting when he'd have to let go.

Phenotypic

The boy, three years old, alone and asleep in the backseat of the car. It's a warm night in June, and the windows are rolled down to let the slight breeze, heavy with the scent of honeysuckle and mown grass, stir wisps of his hair. The car is parked in the driveway of the Steiners, who live four doors down. Only two minutes ago, his parents left the car. They were driving home from a party—a colleague of his father had been celebrating the publication of a book—and they stopped when they saw the lights of the Steiner house. The Steiners had been out of town for a month, and the boy's parents were happy to see that their friends were finally back home, as they were their best friends—their only friends—in this backwoods Texas town that was home to only two things of note: a slaughterhouse and a third-rate college. Since it was late and their son was asleep, they only intended to say a quick hello, not going any farther than the porch, but the Steiners just *had* to show them what they'd brought back from their first trip to England. The boy's parents looked back at the car, though there was no way they could see him in the dark, and then they looked at each other. He's fine, they agreed. Only for a minute, they said.

A teenager's pickup rumbles past, waking the boy. He's slow to come out of his sleep. He breathes deeply, opens his eyes, blinks. He doesn't notice that his parents are missing from the front seat. His attention is drawn instead to the movement of shapes across the roof of the car. What he sees are the shadows of maple leaves cast by the streetlight's reflection in a puddle of water left by Mr. Steiner's sprinkler, but to him they look like the fluttering wings of bats hovering above him. He calls out for Mommy, and it's only when he gets no response that he understands that he's alone, and that something's wrong.

When his parents finally return, having been delayed by too many photographs of Big Ben and Westminster Abbey, they find him shrieking, gasping for breath, choking. His face is slick with snot and tears. It takes them ten minutes to calm him, to convince him that he's safe.

The boy is four years old now. He's wearing OshKosh B'Gosh overalls and his favorite green shirt. He's riding his tricycle down the sidewalk, pumping his legs as furiously as is possible for a boy his age. Up ahead, he sees something dark lying on the cement. He slows to a stop. It's a baby bird, gray and featherless. He climbs from his tricycle and crouches down to examine it. Its eyes are like purple peas beneath their lids. He looks up at the branches of the tree in search of a nest, and there it is: a woven bowl of twigs high above his head. He knows what has happened; the baby bird fell from its nest and died. Maybe it tried to fly too soon.

He doesn't want to touch it with his finger, so he pokes its head with a twig. It doesn't mind; he knows the bird is dead. This fact neither saddens nor scares him, though he does wish that the ants would leave it alone. He understands death. He knows that all living things eventually stop living, and when this happens their bodies break apart and stink and turn back into dirt, which is what all living things are made of. He doesn't know how his eyes and hair and fingernails could all be made of dirt, but his father told him this, so it's true.

He climbs back onto his tricycle. But instead of continuing on his way to the corner (which is as far as his mother will let him go), he rolls back several feet and then pedals over the baby bird. He doesn't know why he does this, but he immediately regrets it. He can't look away from what he's done. Its body is split open like a smushed plum. Its beak, now open, cries out in quiet pain. He knows it doesn't matter—the bird doesn't know that its macaroni insides are now on the outside—but he feels sick. Bad. Guilty. He wishes he could tell the bird that he's sorry for what he's done—it looks so much worse now than it did before—but it's too late.

Crying, he pedals home.

The boy is six years old. He's lying under a blanket on the floorboard of the backseat because he likes how the car, just inches above the road rushing so fast below, hums through his bones. It's the day after Christmas, and they're driving home from his grandfather's house in St. Louis, the house his father grew up in. Though he can't see them in the front, he can hear them whispering just above the whining of a sad violin on the radio. He's only now woken up.

His father's whisper comes from right above him: "I don't care. I've had it. The way he still talks about me . . . the way he ridicules what I do!"

"Quiet," the boy's mother whispers.

"You didn't even hear what he said when I made the mistake of trying to tell him about my book."

The boy hears sounds that remind him of the sounds that he makes right before he cries, but he knows that that's not what he's hearing because his Daddy doesn't cry. Daddies *never* cry.

"You know that he's proud of you," his mother says. "He just doesn't understand."

"Maybe when he's rotting away in a nursing home I'll give him a chance to apologize for talking to me like that."

"But what about Leon? You can't think only of yourself."

"Who do you think I'm thinking of? Why should I continue to expose him to that poison? He's old enough now for that nastiness to start affecting him. His snide comments . . . about me, about what I do. . . ."

"But it's not like you can just cut him off because you—"

"Just watch me."

Though he can't see her, the boy looks toward his mother's seat, waiting for her to respond. He doesn't know quite what is going on, but he knows that he doesn't like the sad and angry sound of his father's voice, quiet as it is. All he knows is that he loves Grandpa, and he doesn't like how his father is talking about him. He looks up and sees his mother peering over the back of her seat at him.

"My, you took a long nap," she says.

He can tell from her eyes that she's wondering whether he's been listening. He closes his eyes again, as if he came out of his sleep for only just a second. He keeps them shut and breathes heavily, hoping that they'll keep talking. He wants to hear his father again, hear him sound normal again, not sad, not angry, hear him talk about how fun Christmas was, but the boy hears nothing but the whirring of the tires over the road and the low crackle of the radio as the violin fades away.

The boy is eleven years old. He's small for his age, just as he's always been small for his age. It's a phrase that he's heard all his life.

His first day in middle school is now over, and having learned only this morning that it's a Stephen F. Austin tradition for the eighth-graders to jump the sixth-graders every day after school for the first week, he's pedaling his bike home as fast as he can, hoping to make up the time he lost while trying in vain to get his locker open after his last class.

In the lunch line, he heard one eighth-grader say to another, "It's our turn now, boy. They better watch out for me, that's all I'm saying. I'm gonna knock me some heads."

The boy looks over his shoulder. Nobody is behind him, but he knows this means nothing. He heard that the shop teacher and the gym coach like to let the eighth-graders out early so they can get a head start. He heard that, after the last bell, the toughest of the eighth-graders convene at a secret location where they've accumulated a stockpile of nunchucks, Chinese throwing stars, and bike chains.

Four more turns to go before he makes it to safety. As his

legs, burning now, pump and pull against the pedals, he rehearses what he'll say if he's jumped (the sound of the word in his head makes his stomach quiver and constrict as he imagines a cluster of bodies dropping upon him from a tree). He'll say he's a seventh-grader who just moved here from Colorado. His father got a job at Texas Instruments.

"I'm supposed to be in eighth grade," he'll add, "but I flunked a year."

When he reaches his house, he runs rubber-legged and lightheaded to the front door, leaving his bike on its side in the grass, its wheels still spinning. Grateful to have safely made it, he collapses on the living room floor, heaving for breath.

But then he remembers that tomorrow is only Tuesday.

The boy is fifteen years old. It's July, and he's sitting behind the wheel of a maroon Buick Regal. The sun is a dusty starburst on the windshield. Mrs. Wilonsky is sitting next to him, wearing a sleeveless blouse that accentuates the saggy heft of her arms. Cindy Watson and Joel Broadaxe are in the backseat. No one says anything. They're all waiting for him. After three weeks of blurry worksheets, dull lectures, and DMV films from the sixties, it's his first day in the driver's seat. Cindy and Joel have already driven through the pylon-marked course in the parking lot. Neither hit a single cone.

"Whenever you're ready," Mrs. Wilonsky says to him, but he hardly hears her. All he can think of is how angry he is at his father for having refused to take him out to practice on the neighborhood streets like everyone else's father.

"That's what Driver's Education is for," his father said. "To learn how to drive. Until you have your learner's permit, it's illegal for me to let you behind the wheel."

But I'm going to look like an idiot!"

"Don't you think you're overstating things a bit?"

"No, I don't."

"Well, your teacher won't think so, and that's all that's

important."

The boy puts the car in gear and slowly presses the gas pedal. The engine whines, but the car doesn't move. He presses the gas pedal harder.

"Take your left foot off the brake, hon," Mrs. Wilonsky says. "There's no reason for you ever to use your left foot when driving an automatic."

A snorting laugh comes from the backseat.

When he lifts his foot from the brake, the tires catch with a squeal, and the car lurches forward over two pylons before jolting to a stop, snapping him hard against the taut seatbelt.

"If we'd been on an actual street and I hadn't been there to save you"—she points down at the car's second brake pedal, the one on her side—"you would've just had yourself a wreck."

"Yes, ma'am," the boy says, embarrassed. He's shaking.

"Just take a breath and settle down now," Mrs. Wilonsky says. "You're acting like you've never been behind the wheel of a car before."

"I think he gave me whiplash, Mrs. Wilonsky," Joel says.

When the boy finally starts rolling forward, he ignores the scraping sound of the pylon caught somewhere underneath them, but Mrs. Wilonsky makes him stop, get out, and pull it free.

The boy is sixteen years old now. He's in the tiny backseat of Brian Clem's Trans Am. Betsy Farmer is sitting next to him. She's looking out the window, watching Brian and Darla Martindale walking toward the dark, woody depths of Ranch 111 Park. He doesn't know what to do, so he just watches her watch. This night started with Brian wanting to check out the lame city fair since there were no good movies playing at Northcross, but it turned into something different as soon as they ran into Darla and Betsy. Then it turned into something even more different—maybe his very first date ever—once he handed Betsy the tiny teddy bear that he somehow won at the ring-toss.

It's so quiet. A gust of wind whistles through the window

that Brian left cracked, stirring the balloon that Darla tied to the radio's knob.

Betsy smiles at him, but he can tell that she's nervous, too. He wonders what she's thinking. Does she want him to kiss her? Or does she want him to continue doing nothing? *Does* he want to kiss her? He doesn't know. She's not ugly, he supposes—he's just never given her much thought before. She's always been one of those faceless girls who doesn't draw much attention to herself, who doesn't raise her hand in class, who isn't a teacher's pet, who doesn't pass notes or talk when she isn't supposed to. She sits quietly, pays attention, and tries. He wonders how someone like her could have a friend like Darla, but then he realizes that people probably wonder the same thing about him and Brian. He wonders if, before now, she's ever given *him* much thought.

It's too quiet. He reaches between the front seats and unties the balloon from the radio's knob. He remembers a funny scene in a movie that he and Brian saw on cable recently: a football player sucked helium at a party and made everyone laugh when he started talking. "I want to grease down and slide all over your body like a snake," the guy said, sounding like a mouse. After picking at the balloon's knot for almost a full minute, the boy finally undoes it and raises the opening to his mouth. The helium rushes coolly down his throat. Realizing that he should have thought of something clever to say before doing this, and afraid that the helium will lose its effect before he comes up with anything, he repeats what the football player said. He can't believe how bizarre his voice sounds. Expecting her to think this is funny, he looks up at her. She's not smiling. In fact, she looks frightened. Her mouth opens, but nothing comes out.

"That's from a movie," he says hurriedly, his voice still high and peeping. "I didn't mean—"

Betsy clutches at the passenger-side door, opening it. The dome light snaps on, illuminating her pale, freckled face, her chapped lips. When she shuts the door behind her, the light clicks off, leaving him alone in the dark.

"Stupid," he says over and over until his voice gradually sinks back to normal. "Stupid, stupid."

The boy is older now—a man—and he's the father of a boy fifteen seconds old. Of course the boy has been alive much longer, but now, finally, he's being thrust out into the air and light and noise. His clock has officially started; the nurse is writing down his time of birth while he writhes in the doctor's extracting hands like a sea-slick eel.

The boy's father—*our* boy, you understand—is all in mint green: V-necked top, pants, booties, hairnet, and surgical mask. He's supposed to have the video camera out and rolling, but he's forgotten. He has *completely* forgotten. In fact, he's completely forgotten everything. He's forgotten the previous twenty-two hours of labor, the screams and the animal grunts, the sweating and the cursing. He's forgotten his ineffective attempts at utilizing what he learned in Lamaze class, the calm counting and the model breathing. He's forgotten his many trips down the hall to retrieve cups of ice chips. He's forgotten the recent death of his mother, and that he agreed to be the one to cut through the umbilical cord. He's forgotten that his father's in the waiting room reading yet another book on Edmund Spenser. He's even forgotten the embarrassment he felt upon first seeing his wife's swollen genitals illuminated so brightly by the lamp pulled down from the ceiling.

No, all that he's aware of is that he's staring at his surprisingly enormous son, his vernix-smeared son. A week ago, he learned that vernix is what the cream cheese stuff covering newborns is called, and he smiled upon discovering this, and whispered, "Vernix, vernix," memorizing it, except that he's forgotten this, too.

What else he's forgotten: the shadows of fluttering bats, the crushed baby bird, his father's tears, his cowardice, his shame, his cowardice, his cowardice.

All that he's aware of is the purple, angry face of his son. His son, who will be *of* him, yes, but *not* him. No, *not* him, not *ever.*

Acknowledgments

These stories originally appeared in the following publications, often in different form: "The New Father," *The Southern Review*; "The Leaves, They Pirouette," *Hayden's Ferry Review*; "The Limits of Adequacy" (as "Motility"), *Five Chapters*; "Horsehead Crossing," *Pank*; "Sub Rosa," *Fiction*; "Congee," *Lo-Ball*; "A Good Son," *Blue Mesa Review*; "Out Here in the Fields (Again)," *Upstreet*; "The Fading of Whittier" (as "Domus Senis"), *Descant*; "With the Snow," *The Distillery: Artistic Spirits of the South*; and "Welcome," *Sou'wester.*

Thanks to the following editors for accepting several of these stories for their journals: Bret Lott, Mark Mirsky, David Daley, Doug Powell and T.J. DiFrancesco, Adrian Matejka and Valerie Vogrin, Skye Pratt, M. Bartley Seigel, Inman Majors, Vivian Dorsel, Salima Keegan, and James A . Moore.

Erin McKnight, thank you for wanting to make this collection see the light of day as a book, and thank you for your tireless effort to make it happen.

For their friendship, support, and inspiration, thanks to Scott Blackwood, Darren DeFrain, Chris Haven, Jon Luthro, Bryan Narendorf, and Jeff Utzinger.

For their guidance, and so much more, enormous thanks to Tom Grimes and Debra Monroe.

For their love and never-ending encouragement, thanks to my parents, Clyde Grauke and Gay Grauke, and my sister, Heather Grauke Cannon.

Thanks to the Grauke and McLaughlin clans, as well as to Patti Collins, David Collins, Diana Ellis, and Charles Ellis.

Thank you, Barb Rodman, Carol Cook Harrell, Evan Carton, and Alan Whiteside.

Kevin Harty, thank you for everything that you've done for me over the last eight years.

I'm also very grateful to La Salle University, the institution and its people, especially those in the Department of English.

To my kids, Eleanor and Peter: thank you both for being such wonderful excuses not to write.

And, finally, I owe my biggest debt of gratitude to my loving wife, Catherine, whose faith in me has always sustained me.

Catherine Collins

Kevin Grauke's fiction has appeared in numerous literary journals, including *The Southern Review*, *Fiction*, *Story Quarterly*, *Quarterly West*, *Five Chapters*, and *Hayden's Ferry Review*. He has an MFA in fiction writing from Texas State University and a PhD in American literature from the University at Buffalo (SUNY). Born and raised in Texas, Kevin now lives in Philadelphia with his wife and two children. He teaches at La Salle University.

CPSIA information can be obtained at www.ICGtesting.com
Printed in the USA
LVOW120951210413
330125LV00003B/89/P

9 781938 466038